Teeline

GOLD

The Course Book

Jean Clarkson

Stephanie Hall

Celia Osborne

Ulli Parkinson

General editor:
Meriel Bowers

HEINEMANN
EDUCATIONAL

Heinemann Educational Publishers
Halley Court, Jordan Hill, Oxford OX2 8EJ
Part of Harcourt Education

Heinemann is the registered trademark
of Harcourt Education Limited

Complete work © Harcourt Education Limited
© Teeline outlines: Teeline Education Ltd 1991
First published 1991
06 07 24 23 22

British Library Cataloguing in Publication Data

Teeline gold
1. Shorthand
I. Bowers, Meriel
653.428

10-digit ISBN 0 435453 53 X
13-digit ISBN 978 0 435453 53 4

Typeset by Fakenham Photosetting Ltd, Fakenham, Norfolk

Printed and bound in the UK by Scotprint

Other Teeline titles available
Teeline Gold: **Workbook** by Harry Butler
Teeline Gold: **Speed Ladder** by Meriel Bowers and Stephanie Hall
Teeline Gold: **Speed Ladder Workbook** by Harry Butler
Teeline Word List by I. C. Hill
Teeline Word Groupings by George Hill
New Teeline Dictation Book edited by George Hill
Teeline Shorthand Dictation Passages by Dorothy Bowyer
Handbook for Teeline Teachers edited by Harry Butler
Medical Teeline by Pat Garner and Pat Clare

Contents

Preface

Teeline is a modern shorthand system invented by James Hill. It is noted for its simplicity and ease of learning, and also for the high speeds which its writers achieve.

Teeline is fun to learn – copying and repetition are not regarded as chores but as integral parts of the learning process. You will soon see how few basic rules there are to be learnt and how quickly and easily new learning can be mastered.

The beauty of Teeline is its flexibility; there may be several equally correct outlines for one word. However, while you are still a beginner it is better to stick to the textbook rules and outlines. Once you have a thorough understanding of the system you can adapt it to your own needs. As you build your knowledge so you can begin to build up a repertoire of abbreviating devices which will really increase your speed.

Theory learning is simply a means to an end – the winged art of taking dictation at increasing speeds which the writer is able to read without difficulty or hesitation.

Meriel Bowers
1991

Acknowledgements

The authors and publishers would like to thank I C Hill and M Bowers for permission to use material from *Teeline Revised Edition*. They also acknowledge the considerable support given to Teeline over the years by Mrs I C Hill and Mrs J M Brown, both directors of Teeline Education Ltd.

The vocabulary used in Teeline Gold has been based on data from the COBUILD English Language research project at the University of Birmingham, copyright William Collins Sons & Co Ltd.

All the Teeline shorthand outlines in this book have been written by Stephanie Hall, to whom thanks are due.

Introduction

Getting started

Now that you have a copy of *Teeline: The Course Book*, you should also go out and buy yourself either a small notebook or (preferably) an alphabetically-indexed book such as an address book. You will use this to note down important vocabulary, special outlines and word groupings. You can then easily identify items to practise.

You will also need a spiral-bound, ruled notebook in which to write your shorthand. Before you use it, rule a left-hand margin of 2–3 cm throughout the book. This space is for inserting instructions, alterations and corrections. When using the book use only the front sheets until the notebook has been worked through, then turn it round and use the backs of the sheets.

You will need a pencil or ball-point pen for writing. Unlike other shorthand systems you do not need a special pen – choose whatever you feel most comfortable with. However, if you are using a pencil make sure it is sharp and whatever you are using make sure you have a spare to hand when you are taking dictation.

Teeline

Teeline is based on handwriting – your own handwriting – so the slope, shape and size will be personal to you. However, just as you can read other people's handwriting, and they yours, so you can read the outlines in this book and copy from them.

Of course, everyone's Teeline will differ in size, but if you write your outlines too big, or too small, this may hinder your speed (and shorthand is all about writing quickly). Keep the letters in good proportion to each other, trying to get 10–14 outlines on a line. The outlines in this book are a good size to aim at.

Using this book

Whenever a new theory point is introduced there are examples of how to write the outline. Practise writing the outlines until you feel comfortable with them.

Whenever you write a word, always say it to yourself. This helps you to associate the outline with the sound and will become your own personal dictating system.

There is a set of exercises after each new piece of theory to help you assimilate it. Read these several times, each more quickly than the time before then write the shorthand saying the words to yourself as you write them. Finally, try taking the exercises as dictation. Practise reading back your outlines once you have written them.

After the theory in each unit are a number of 'special outlines'. These are shortened versions of frequently occurring words. It is well worth the time and effort to learn these because they really will help you to increase the speed at which you write Teeline.

Each unit concludes with three longer dictation passages. Practise reading these too. An instant recognition of outlines is a positive way to develop your speed. If you are working on your own get a friend to dictate the material to you – or better still make an audio cassette to play through your personal stereo. The longhand is at the back of this book and is counted in 10s so that you can work out your dictation speed.

Always check your outlines and correct any that are wrong. Remember that in Teeline there may be several equally correct ways to write something. The outlines in this book, however, are the most acceptable forms.

It is not necessary to work through all the exercises in each unit. If you feel confident you have mastered the theory you can move on to the next unit. However, it is not possible to skip a unit as they present the theory in a continuous and systematic way.

If you do leave out some exercises, make a note of which ones and go back later to use them for revision.

Transcription
Do make the effort to type back your Dictation Practice. After all, shorthand is only a means to an end and that end is usually a memo, letter or article. Date the piece and display it as you would in an examination or at work.

Support material
Teeline Gold: *The Workbook* will give you additional practice material. It has been specially written to accompany this book.

To follow on from *The Course Book* – to extend your vocabulary, give you additional groupings and build your speed ready for the world of work – move up to Teeline Gold: *Speed Ladder*.

Heinemann Educational has many other Teeline titles to support your learning needs.

Teeline is a fast writing system using adapted longhand letters, which is why Teeline is so simple to learn. In order to write faster than normal handwriting would permit, the Teeline system streamlines the writing of the letters. The Teeline letters take their position from the longhand equivalent, ie G, J, P and Q cut the line, T is written above the line as in the small cross stroke of a handwritten t, and the other letters sit on the line. Vowels have two forms known as the full vowel and the indicator, which are all written smaller than consonants. The Teeline system removes all unnecessary letters within a word to increase writing speed.

Try to keep your Teeline small and neat. The Teeline in this book is a good example.

The Teeline alphabet

	Longhand	Teeline letter	Indicator	
A	A	A		Taken from the top of a capital **A**.
B	B	6		A streamlined ...
C	c	c		Same letter as in longhand. C also represents **CK** as in the word **back**.
D		—		A short dash written on the line.
E	E			Bottom part of a capital **E**.
F	f	or		Part of a handwritten .... It can be written upwards or downwards. When **PH** or **GH** have the sound of **F** (as in **enough**, **phone**), then letter **F** is used.
G	g			A simplified form of a handwritten ... . Letter **G** also represents **DGE**, as in **edge**, where the **D** is silent.

H	H		The downstroke of a capital **H**, *always* written downwards.
I	*i*		The handwritten ...*i*..... is streamlined into a small sharply angled sign and the dot is omitted. The indicator is generally written downwards, but in order to get a sharper outline, it is occasionally written upwards.
J	*j*		The dot is removed from ....*j*...... and the tail smoothed out.
K	K		Part of the capital **K**, written as a continuous stroke.
L	*l*	or	The downstroke of a handwritten ..*l*....... . The abbreviated second form is sometimes written upwards.
M	*m*		The initial hook and middle stem of a handwritten ..*m*.... are removed, leaving only a wide arch, written from left to right.
N	*n*		The first hook of a handwritten ....*n*.... .
O	O	O	Full **O** is used in only a few special cases, instead the indicator is used, which is the shallow under-section of **O**, written from left to right.
P	*p*		The downstroke of a handwritten **P**, written through the line when it begins a word, but *always* written downwards.

QU			English words never contain a **Q** standing alone. Teeline letter **Q** is the loop, which in longhand joins the **Q** and U together,

...This is written through the line in its longhand position. |

R		The first stroke of the old cursive handwritten ..., which is *always* written upwards.

S		A small circle taken from the handwritten ..., and which may be written in the most convenient direction.

T		The cross-stroke of a handwritten/printed **t**. When standing alone, or with only a vowel or an **S** before it, it is placed above the writing line, whereas **D**, which is the same length, is written on it.

U		A small and narrow version of a capital **U**. The indicator for **U** is reduced to one side stroke, which is the same as one of the **E** indicators, although they will never be confused in context.

V		The capital form of **V** is retained and must be kept upright, so as not to confuse it with **I**.

W		The middle stem of a handwritten ...... is removed to form one single curve, written from left to right.

X		The capital form of **X** is kept. Usually it is better if ...... is written first.

Y ..**y**.. ..**u**.......... A written **Y** without the loop.

Z ..**z ʒ** ..**9**........ Derived from a handwritten **Z**.

Copy the letters of the alphabet, saying the letters as you write them. When copying try to keep the outlines the same size. Follow the direction of writing the letters as shown by the arrows. Remember to write the vowels smaller than the consonants.

Commonly words represented by letters of the alphabet

To make writing even quicker, frequently used words are written in a shortened form. The following Teeline letters represent commonly occurring words:

A	..**∧**....	able/ability/able to	N	..**1**....	and
	..****....	a	P	..**|**....	pence/page
B	..**6**....	be/been	Q	..**U**...	question/equal
D	..**━**....	do/day	R	..**╱**....	are
E	..**┗**....	electric	S	..**ℓ**....	south
F	..**∅**....	from	T	..**━**....	to
G	..**ʒ**....	go	U	..**ʋ**....	you
H	..**ℓ**....	he	V	..**Y**....	very
I	..**ʀ**....	I/eye	W	..**ᴗ**....	we
K	..**ᐸ**....	kind	X	..**✗**....	accident
L	..**ℓ**....	letter	Y	..**ᴜ**....	your
M	..**⌒**....	me			

Write out these words until you feel you really know them. Say the words to yourself each time you write them. Saying the words is important because you must come to associate *hearing* the word with *writing* the symbol if your eventual aim is to take dictation.

Exercise 1.1

From memory, write the following words in Teeline. Then check the outlines against the ones shown above and correct any you did not remember.

able	a	do	from	he	been
letter	and	question	south	you	we

Exercise 1.2

From memory, write the following words in Teeline. Then check and correct as in the last exercise.

be	a	electric	go	eye
kind	me	pence	are	to
very	accident	your		

Transcription

Writing back or typing back from shorthand is known as transcription. Teeline words are known as outlines and are read from left to right and top to bottom. The Teeline system is based on spelling, although occasionally phonetics (sounds) are used.

Exercise 1.3

Practise writing the following simple words in Teeline. As you will see they all start with a vowel indicator, followed by the next letter joined to it.

am	an	as	if	in	is	it

Exercise 1.4

Here are some more outlines made up of two letters joined together. Copy down the Teeline and write the longhand word next to it.

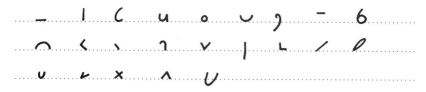

Always remember to check your work and make any necessary corrections.

Exercise 1.5

Revision   Transcribe the following words.

Once again remember to check your work and make any necessary corrections.

Joining letters

Letters are joined together as they are in handwriting. The second letter generally begins where the first ends using one movement, the pen not being lifted from the page (except for writing **K** and **X** – see page 8).

Reduction of words

Rd yr Tln n rt it evry da n u wl sn imprv.

If you can read this sentence you are part way to learning the principles of Teeline. When writing Teeline shorthand words are reduced to a 'skeleton' by removing all unnecessary letters in order to make a shorter written outline.

Remove all medial vowels

It is not necessary to write vowels which occur in the middle of words (medial vowels), for example:

hear is reduced to hr and written .. 𝑉 ....

week is reduced to wk and written . 𝖴 ....

pen is reduced to pn and written .. ↳ ....

Sometimes medial vowels may be written to make an easier outline or to avoid confusion in reading back, such as:

big	job	bend	ban

It is very rare that this is necessary because usually the meaning of what you are writing will tell you what the word is. *But* time ....

and not . 𝖳 .... are safer with the vowel.

Remove all silent letters

Letters which are not sounded are omitted.

In the word **take** the **e** is silent and now the word is reduced to tk

and written 

light is reduced to lt and written 

walk is reduced to wk and written 

dumb is reduced to dm and written 

cough is reduced to cf and written 

Remove one of double letters

When double letters occur in words only one needs to be written.

tell is reduced to tl and written 

bill is reduced to bl and written 

little is reduced to ltl and written 

add is reduced to ad and written 

Exercise 2.1

Read the following exercise from which all unnecessary letters have been removed.

Emplyrs expct aplcnts fr scrtrl psts t b skld in al aspcts o ofc wrk, incldng shrthnd, tpng, wrd prcsng and ofc prcdrs.

Tln is esy t rd n rt n fn to lrn. U mst undrstnd, hvr, tht as wl as rtng Tln as qcly as u cn, u mst trnscrb yr shrthnd nts spdly n acrtly. Alws hv a dctnry on yr dsk n us it.

At the beginning of a word the first letter is usually written in its normal writing position. When a word starts with a small letter or a vowel followed by a longer letter it is a good idea, in order to avoid writing too far below the line, to write the second letter in its normal writing position.

cab  kept 

There are two letters you can only write by lifting the pen: **X** which
is written just like normal longhand and **K** when it follows **H**, **J** or
P as in:

hook   joke   peak

Exercise 2.2

After crossing out all unnecessary letters, write the Teeline outline
for each of the following words.

told	poor	live	man	year
level	keep	accept	pass	voice
role	hike	damage	tough	give

Exercise 2.3

Read these Teeline letters, copy them neatly and then see if you can
read and make as many words as possible from your own outlines.

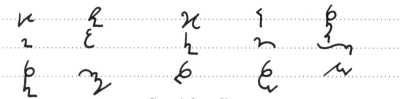

Special outlines

To speed up writing many frequently used words can be reduced to
make a shorter outline. These special outlines should be learned as
they appear in each unit and regular practice will help to increase
your writing speed.

Examples of special outlines

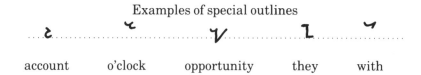

account   o'clock   opportunity   they   with

In many cases of frequently occurring long words the normal
longhand abbreviation may be used, for example:

company → co   representative → rep   etcetera → etc

Remember: Teeline is a flexible system of shorthand and full outlines may be used, if preferred.

Exercise 2.4

Transcribe (ie read and write or type) the following simple sentences. A full-stop is represented by a long sloping line written upwards, ⟋ and a question mark by the usual symbol.

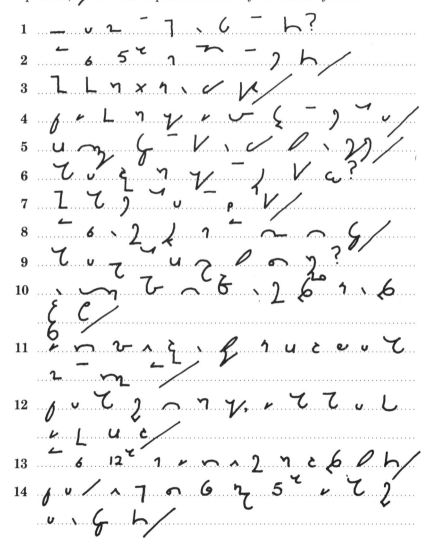

Additional Teeline characters

In addition to the normal alphabet, the following Teeline characters are used to represent letter combinations. Two of them also represent words.

CH	CH sign	C is attached to **H** and the sign written on the line in the **H** position.
WH	WH sign	**W** is joined to **H** and written on the line in the **H** position.
TH *and* **the**	TH sign	**T** is joined to **H** and written on the line in the **H** position.
SH *and* **shall**	S sign	The letter **S** is used to represent **SH.**

Exercise 3.1

Read the following sentences:

1 ....

2 ....

3 ....

4 ....

5 ....

You will notice that in words such as **purchase** or **path** where **CH** and **TH** follow other letters the first letter is written in its normal position and the rest follows on. Lightly sounded letters such as the **T** in the word **Dutch** can be safely omitted.

Letters WH

In words beginning with **WH** the **H** is usually included to give a clearer outline.

when	where	while	who	why

NB In 'while' the abbreviated form of **L** is written upwards.
In 'why' the **Y** is replaced by an **I** indicator, also written upwards.

Vowels

Vowels are smaller than consonants. The indicator is more commonly used and it should be one third the size of other letters.

a   o

e   u

i

When a vowel is the first letter of a word it *must* be shown. Similarly, when there is a vowel at the end of a word that has a definite sound it *must* be shown.

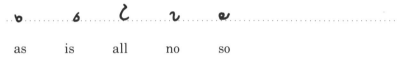

as	is	all	no	so

Vowel indicators should be used if there is any likelihood of confusion when reading back (see Unit 2). They are written next to the stroke to which they relate. However, this is *very rarely* necessary.

Heavy sounds use the full vowel, light sounds the indicator.

ship	shape	shop	chip	cheap	man	men

When a word begins or ends with a double vowel, either the first or more strongly sounded vowel is shown.

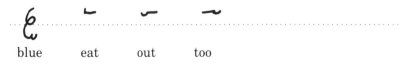

blue	eat	out	too

Exercise 3.2

Read and write the following sentences:

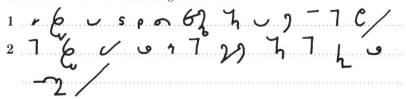

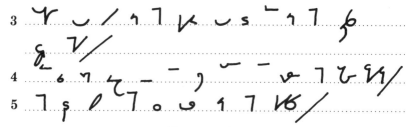

Punctuation

As you learned in the last unit, the Teeline full stop is a long

sloping line written upwards ... ╱ ....

- capitals are indicated by writing two small sloping dashes

  underneath the word, as in: ... 🝆 ... Wales ... ╱ ... Japan

- a Teeline hyphen is the same sign written between the two

  halves of the outlines ...... ⌐ ∶ ⌐ ...... tea-time

- a Teeline dash is ... ◜ ....

- other punctuation marks are as in ordinary writing.

Context

Some words are written with the same outline but the sense of the
sentence generally makes it clear which word is required.

... ⌒ .   could be: late, let, lit, light, lot
          or even: lad, led, lid, load, laid, lead

but if the sentence was 'We shall be ⌒ for work', **late** is the one
word which makes sense.

Reading

If you cannot read a letter or word then read on ahead, and
context usually helps to bring the word to mind. If this does not
help then write the letters out in longhand to form a skeleton eg

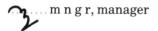 ... m n g r, manager

Special outlines
represented by letters of the alphabet

A above the line .... is **at**

The full outline is contracted by removing the **T**.

O above the line .... is **of**

The full outline is contracted by removing the **F**.

T in its usual position .... is **to**

D in its usual position ...___... is **do** or **day**

So **today** or **to do** are written .... The **D** starts a little to the right of **T** and just underneath it.

Exercise 3.3

Read and write the following sentences:

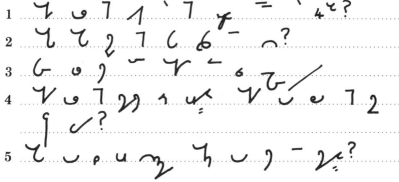

Dictation practice

Read the following sentences and prepare for dictation.

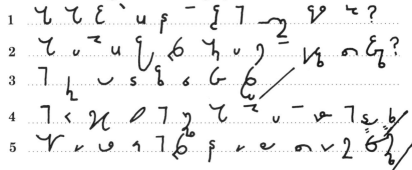

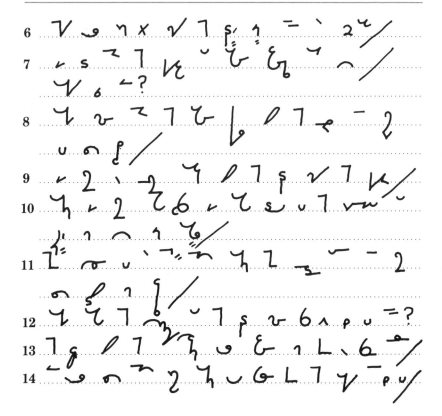

The letter S

The Teeline **S** is a small circle which can be written either clockwise or anti-clockwise.

You will have no problems if you remember two simple rules – it goes *inside* curves and *outside* angles.

For instance:

- It fits inside curved letters.

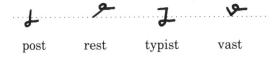

was   less   miss   seem

If you have followed the curve round to tuck in the **S**, you are ready to add more letters.

waste   last   missed   seemed

- When two straight letters meet, join them together by putting the **S** outside the angle where it can be seen clearly.

post   rest   typist   vast

Plurals

Words can be made plural by adding an **S**.

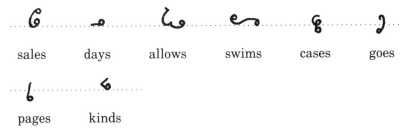

sales   days   allows   swims   cases   goes

pages   kinds

When joining **S** to other letters, choose the way you find easier, and then keep to it.

or		or	
staff		series	
or		or	
test		stops	

S and Z

In most words containing **Z**, it doesn't really matter whether you write an **S** or a **Z**. After all they sound very much alike and when **Z** comes in the middle of a word you can safely use an **S**.
For instance:

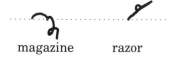

magazine   razor

However, when **Z** *starts* a word, use a **Z**.

zip   zero   zoom

Exercise 4.1

Read and write the following sentences:

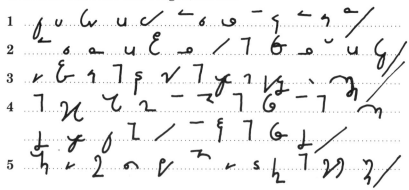

Special outlines

6   8

business   success

Distinguishing outlines

When two or more frequently occurring words have the same outline, it is necessary to give each word a *distinguishing outline* in order to avoid possible errors in transcription.

has ...ᒪ.... the H is sloped in the A direction.

his ...ᒥ.... the H is sloped towards the I.

perhaps ..⋏ᖯ.. the H and the P form a straight line sloped in the A direction

purpose ..⋏ᖯ.. keep the P straight.

amused ⌐ᖚ.... use an S.

amazed ⌐ᖚ.... use a Z.

To show the difference between **this**, **these** and **those** – three words which reduce to the same skeleton outline – write them like this:

this ...ᒥ.... slope it in the I direction.

these ..ᒪ.... keep the H straight in the E direction.

those ...ᒪ.... keep the H straight and put in the vowel.

Exercise 4.2

Read and write the following sentences:

1
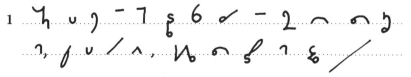

Dictation practice

You are now ready to try your first pieces of dictation, but first read and practise them. Remember you *must* write the full stop signs during dictation.

1 A day in Paris

2 Memo to office managers

Unit 5
Word groupings: 1

To write Teeline at a higher speed, it helps to join together words which are often linked in speech. These are known as **word groupings** – the first word of such a grouping is written in its normal position and the rest of the outline follows. The groupings shown in this unit are examples of what it is possible to do if frequently occurring word patterns join together easily.

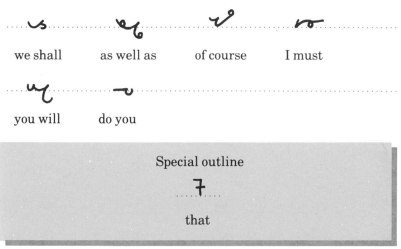

we shall	as well as	of course	I must

you will	do you

Special outline

that

In some word groupings you may *leave out* or *add* letters within the grouping, to make reading/writing easier.

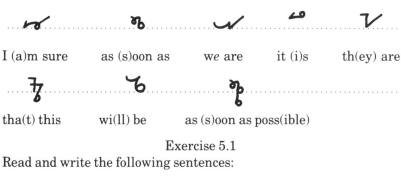

I (a)m sure	as (s)oon as	we are	it (i)s	th(ey) are

tha(t) this	wi(ll) be	as (s)oon as poss(ible)

Exercise 5.1

Read and write the following sentences:

1
2

3 ⟨shorthand outline⟩
4 ⟨shorthand outline⟩ = 7?
5 ⟨shorthand outline⟩

Common words in groupings
Able (to)

The word **able (to)** in word groupings: the vowel sign is disjoined, and is written close to the previous consonant to form part of the outline.

I am able to   ⟨outline⟩   You will be able to   ⟨outline⟩

we are able to   ⟨outline⟩   We should be able to   ⟨outline⟩

we shall be able to ⟨outline⟩   he is able to   ⟨outline⟩

Exercise 5.2
Read and write the following sentences:

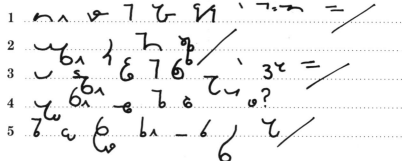

1 ⟨shorthand⟩
2 ⟨shorthand⟩
3 ⟨shorthand⟩
4 ⟨shorthand⟩
5 ⟨shorthand⟩

Special outline – Have

Have ⟨outline⟩ is a blend of H and V, with the **H** stroke sloped to form half of the **V**. In groupings **have** ⟨outline⟩ is used at the beginning, whereas in the middle or at the end of a grouping **have** can be shortened to **V** only.

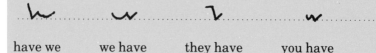

have we   we have   they have   you have

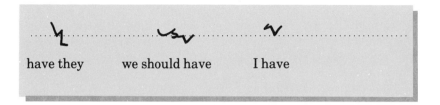

| have they | we should have | I have |

Exercise 5.3
Read and write the following sentences:

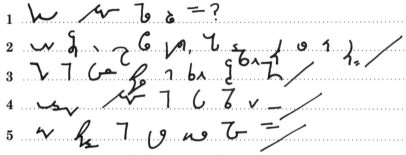

Be/been in word groupings

Letter **B** .. **6** .. representing the word **be**, also represents the word **been** in groupings. The sense of the sentence will tell you which it is.

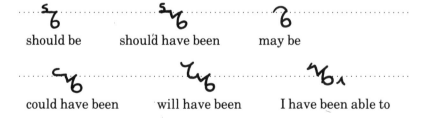

| should be | should have been | may be |

| could have been | will have been | I have been able to |

Exercise 5.4
Read and write the following sentences:

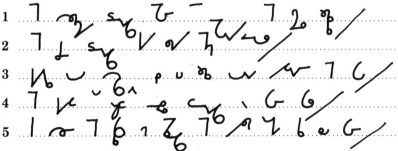

The in word groupings

A very common word in groupings is **the**. In some groupings the full **the** should be written, or it can be reduced to **H** only to give a better join, but *never* use the second form at the beginning of the grouping.

and the ...**ʔ**...   with the ....**ʔ**..   if the ..**ʄ**....

to the ...**ʔ**...   from (t)h(e) ..**ρ**....   of (t)h(e) ...**ʔ**....

by (t)h(e) ..**ρ**...   that (t)h(e) ....**ʔ**..   at (t)h(e) ..**ʔ**.....

all (t)h(e) ...**ʔ**...   to them ...**ʔ**.   at the same (t)ime **ʒ**

Exercise 5.5

Read and write the following sentences:

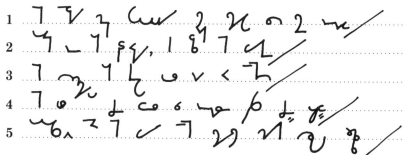

Dictation practice

Read the following passages and prepare for dictation.

1 Opening of hotel

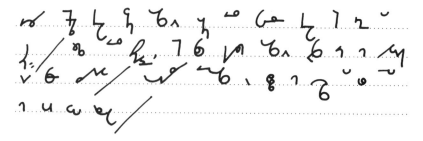

2 Sales notification

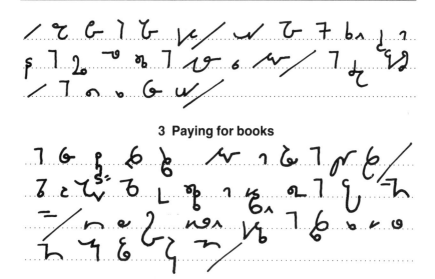

3 Paying for books

Remember: It is not essential to join words into groupings, but by doing so, your speed will increase considerably.

Would in groupings

The word **would** is written ..⌣⌐.. when it stands alone or starts a grouping.

would you	would be	would not	would have

would we be able to

When **would** follows another word, it may be reduced to a small **w** ..⌣.... written below the preceding word in the **D** position.

we would	I would	you would	he would have been able to

it would be

WARD/WORD/WOOD

A small **w** ..⌣.... can also be used as a *word ending*. It is written underneath and close up to the previous part of the outline and the context will make it clear which ending is required.

WARD

upward	homeward	reward	inward

Other letters may be added:

towards	inwards	rewarded

WORD

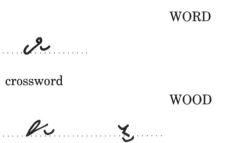

crossword

WOOD

firewood   oakwood

Word in groupings

last word

Exercise 6.1

Read and write the following sentences:

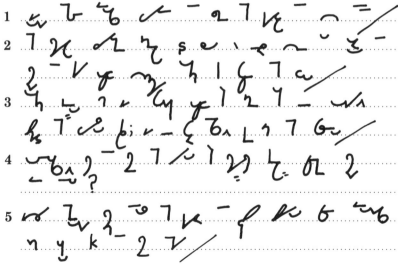

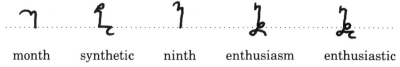

NTH blend

Remember, in groupings **the** can be reduced to **H**, omitting the **T**.
NTH can be shortened in the same way to **NH** ..**ʔ**.. This should be
written with the **H** standing on the line in its normal position.

month   synthetic   ninth   enthusiasm   enthusiastic

Special outline

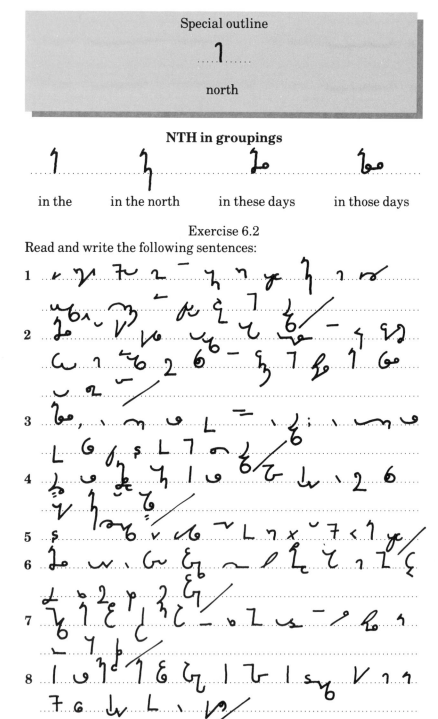

north

NTH in groupings

in the   in the north   in these days   in those days

Exercise 6.2

Read and write the following sentences:

1

2

3

4

5

6

7

8

Dictation practice
Read the following passages and prepare for dictation.

1 Memo to staff

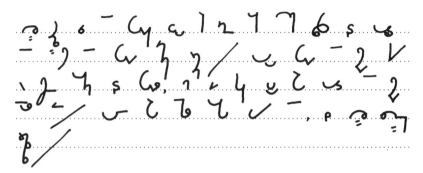

2 Office machinery

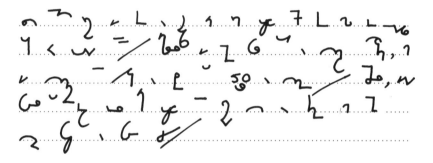

3 Advertisement

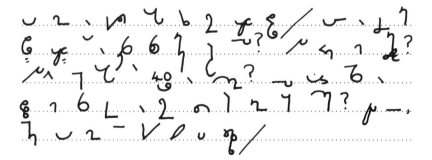

Unit 7
T and D

T is always written *above* the line in the **T** position when standing alone, beginning a word or when preceded by an **S** or a vowel.

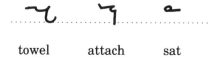

towel   attach   sat

When followed by **P** or **G** write the outline a little lower to give these letters their correct position through the line.

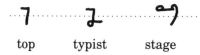

top   typist   stage

To distinguish some words ending in **T** or **D**, the whole word can be written in the **T** or **D** position.

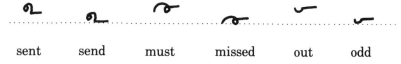

sent   send   must   missed   out   odd

D is always written *on* the line in the **D** position when standing alone, beginning a word or when preceded by an **S** or a vowel.

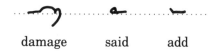

damage   said   add

T and **D** are *never* joined. They are shown together by writing one stroke above or below the other and slightly to the right.

T followed by **T**	tight		total		teeth
T followed by **D**	tied		waited		quoted
D followed by **D**	did		divided		deduce
D followed by **T**	date		dated		detail

Words ending in -day

As we use **D** for day, so words ending in **-day** can be written with a **D** ending.

midday   Sunday   Tuesday

Exercise 7.1

Read and write the following sentences:

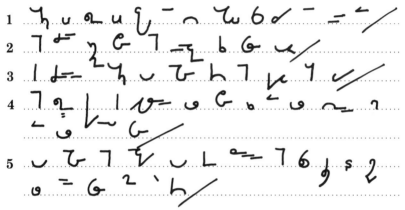

B followed by T or D

When joining **T** to **B**, write the **T** at the top of the **B** circle.

but   rebate   debited

When joining **D** to **B** write the **D** at the bottom of the circle.

beads   robbed   clubbed

C and K, CT and CD

As **C** and **K** are interchangeable except at the beginning of a word, **C** can be written instead of **K** to give a better outline. When the

letters **T** or **D** follow **C**, simply join the two together by lengthening
the **C**.

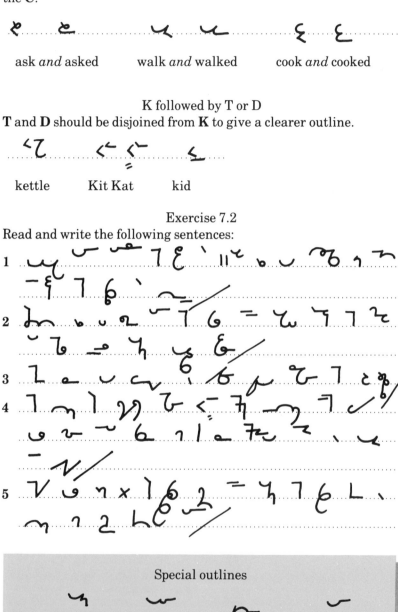

ask *and* asked   walk *and* walked   cook *and* cooked

K followed by T or D

T and **D** should be disjoined from **K** to give a clearer outline.

kettle   Kit Kat   kid

Exercise 7.2

Read and write the following sentences:

1

2

3

4

5

Special outlines

within   without   immediate   what

Word groupings

that day	some day	with us	with you

Exercise 7.3

Read and write the following sentences:

1

2

3

4

5

Dictation practice

Read the following passages and prepare for dictation.

1 Memo to hotel manager

2 Note about missed meeting

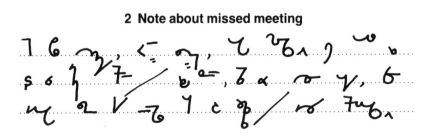

(shorthand outline)

3 Changes in car park

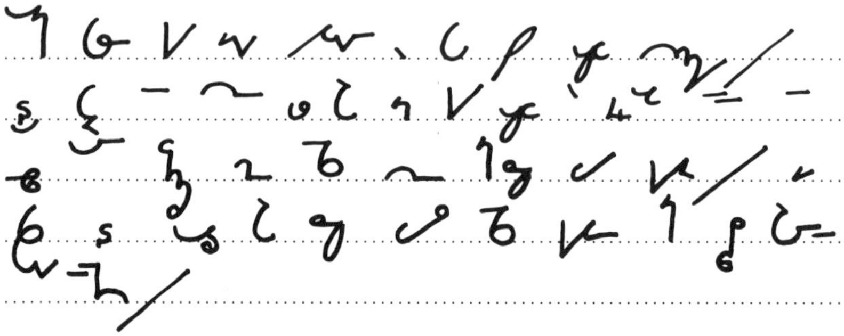

(shorthand outlines)

Unit 8
Y at the end of a word;
Y in the middle of a word

AY at the end of a word

If the last letter of a word is a **Y** but it takes its sound from the preceding **A**, use an **A**.

delay	relay	stay	say	way	Ray

If it sounds like an **A** use an **A** is an easy way of remembering this. To help you in reading back, it is better to use a full **A** after **H**, **M** and **P**.

hay	may	repay

Obey has an **E** in front of the **Y** but in this word it sounds like an **A**. Here again, if it sounds like an **A** use an **A**, **obey**.

Similarly, if a word ending **EY** sounds like an **E** use an **E**. For example, **key**.

I and Y at the end of a word

Some words finish with **IE** and the **E** is silent. Others have **IGH** at the end and the **GH** is not sounded, while others have a **Y** at the end and it sounds like an **I**. In all these cases, if it sounds like an **I** use an **I**. The **I** indicator can be written in either direction to give a good joining.

high	pie	my	guy	buy

Some words finish in a **Y** but sound like an **I**, so you could have:

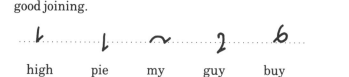

busy	lady	sorry	many

Useful rule: always write the **I** upwards at the end of a word if it comes after **G H M N P** or **SH**. It is important that the **I** is clearly seen.

Exercise 8.1

Read and write the following sentences:

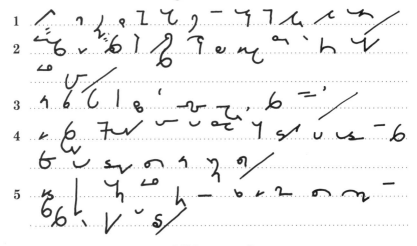

OY in a word

If a word has **OY** in it, use a Teeline **Y**. It makes no difference whether the **OY** comes in the middle or at the end of the word.

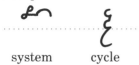

| boy | Roy | royal | joy | loyalty | toys |

Y in the middle of a word

This doesn't happen very often. If the **Y** sounds like an **I** in most cases, as with vowels, you can leave it out. Just occasionally, however, it makes a better letter joining if you put in an **I**, for example:

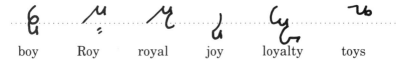

system   cycle

Where **Y** has a distinct sound as in **lawyer** the **Y** must be shown,

Exercise 8.2

Read and write the following sentences:

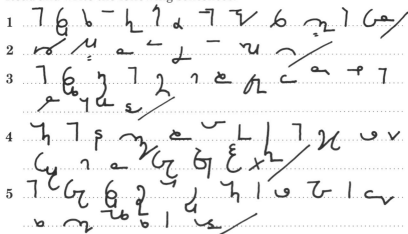

1
2
3
4
5

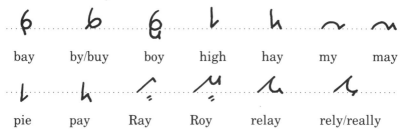

Think about these outlines and ask yourself why they have been written in this way.

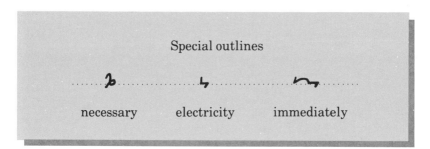

| bay | by/buy | boy | high | hay | my | may |

| pie | pay | Ray | Roy | relay | rely/really |

Special outlines

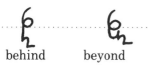

necessary   electricity   immediately

Distinguishing outlines

behind   beyond

Word grouping

I am sorry

Exercise 8.3

Read and write the following sentences:

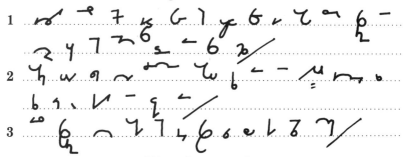

Dictation practice

Read the following passages and prepare for dictation.

1 Problem of unpaid bill

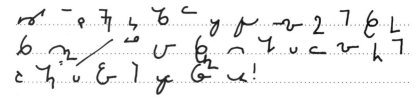

2 Note from headteacher to his assistant

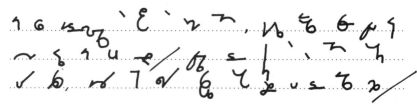

3 Overtime request

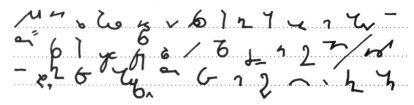

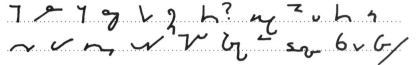

From page 35
Did you look carefully at the outlines on this page? Write the
correct endings as shown and you will have no problem reading
back your outlines.

Unit 9
More about vowels

Vowels at the beginning of words

When a word begins with a vowel, the vowel indicator is generally used.

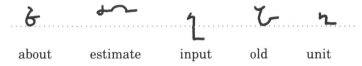

about   estimate   input   old   unit

The full vowel is used if the indicator does not join up well and in some words the indicator can be written upwards.

Letter A

Before **V**, **W** and **X** write the upstroke of full **A**.

avail   average   away   awaited

Before **R** the full vowel **A** is used.

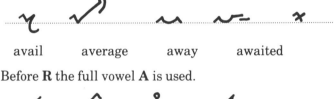

air   area   arise   airy

AU can be represented by indicator **A** at the beginning of a word but, to make reading back easier, the full **A** is often used to give a distinctive outline.

autumn   audio   automatic   August   audited

Exercise 9.1

Read and write the following sentences:

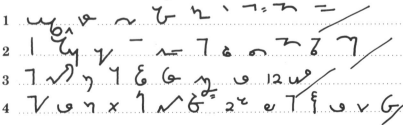

5

Letter E

As the indicator would not show before **P** and **Q**, use the full **E**.

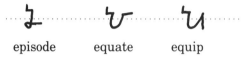

episode   equate   equip

Exercise 9.2

Read and write the following sentences:

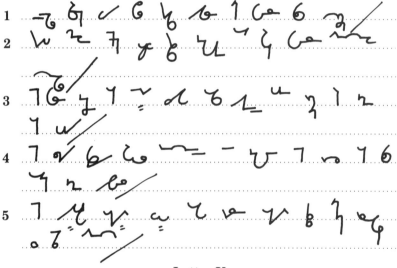

1

2

3

4

5

Letter U

As the indicator would not show before **P**, use the full **U**.

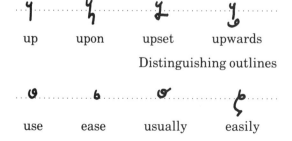

up   upon   upset   upwards

Distinguishing outlines

use   ease   usually   easily

The full **U** represents the heavy sound of **U** at the end of words.

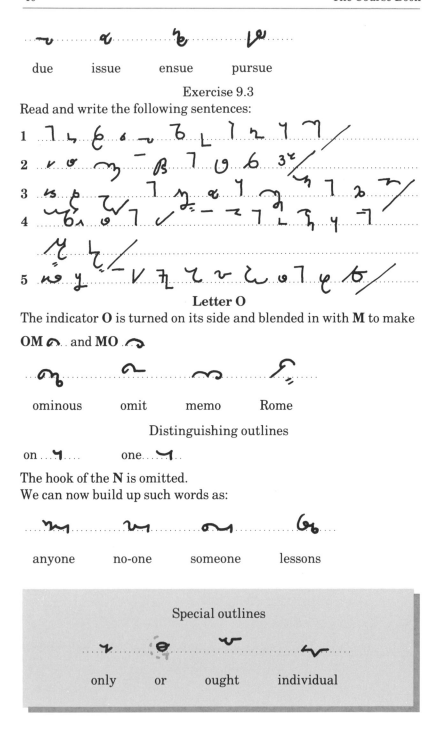

due   issue   ensue   pursue

Exercise 9.3

Read and write the following sentences:

1

2

3

4

5

Letter O

The indicator **O** is turned on its side and blended in with **M** to make

OM ⌒ and **MO** ⌒

ominous   omit   memo   Rome

Distinguishing outlines

on ⌐   one ⌐

The hook of the **N** is omitted.
We can now build up such words as:

anyone   no-one   someone   lessons

Special outlines

only   or   ought   individual

Word grouping

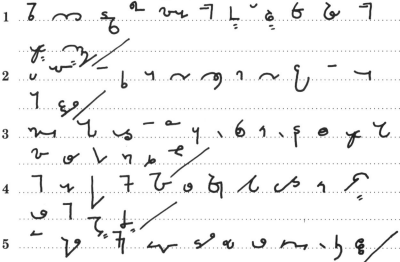

not only

You must make sure that the **ON** blend does not look like a **Y**.

Exercise 9.4

Read and write the following sentences:

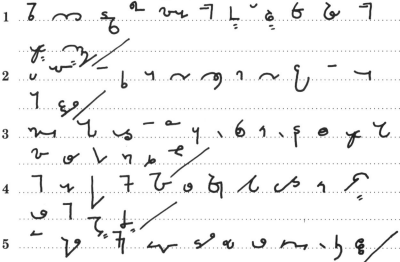

Dictation practice

Read the following passages and prepare for dictation.

1 Installation of lifts

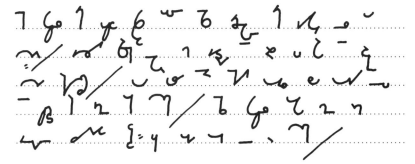

2 Staff Club Account

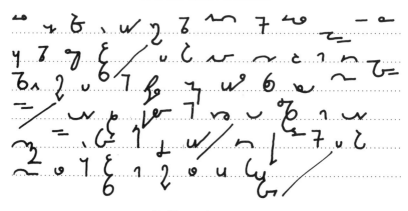

3 Choosing a car

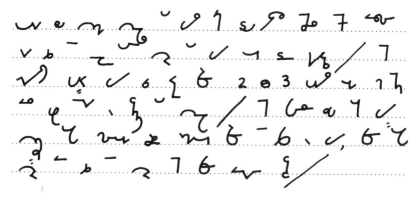

A disjoined vowel indicator is used to represent frequently-used word endings. It is written close to the previous part of the outline and keeps its normal size.

I Indicator for -ING

being	doing	willing	meeting	going

having	saying	ring	needing

if -ING is repeated the indicator is written twice.

ringing	singing	bringing

Other letters may be joined to the indicator.

beings	things	wings	singer	linger	fingers	lingering

In a grouping, **the** may be added to the disjoined indicator. **TH** is written to give a better outline.

taking the	having the	making the

-INGLE
A disjoined **L** is written in the -**ING** position to represent -**INGLE** at the end of a word.

single   mingle   tingle   singles

-INGLY

When a word ends in **-INGLY**, **-LY** is written in the **-ING** position.

charmingly   lovingly   willingly

Exercise 10.1

Read and write the following sentences:

1

2

3

4

5

In the same way, use: **A** indicator for **-ANG**

sang   hang   clang   gangs   tangle   hanger

O indicator for **-ONG**

along   among   belong   longer   wrongly   longhand

U indicator for -UNG

lung	young	rung	rungs	bungle	hungry

E indicator for -ENG (which usually has -TH or -THEN added)

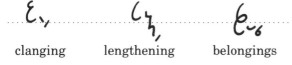

length	lengthen	lengthy

Words may have a combination of indicator endings

clanging	lengthening	belongings

Disjoined vowel indicators are not used when **E** is added to the ending giving the soft sound of **ANGE, ENGE, INGE, ONGE, UNGE**, so we write:

change	hinge	sponge

Exercise 10.2

Read and write the following sentences:

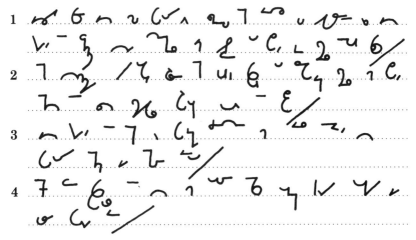

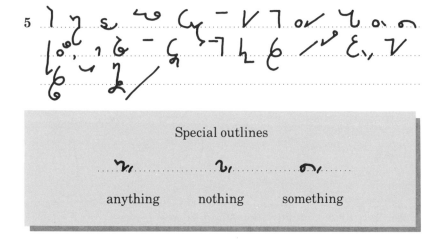

5

Special outlines

anything	nothing	something

Word grouping

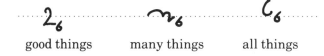

sending you

-ING or **-INGS** can be used for **thing** or **things** in a grouping.

good things	many things	all things

Exercise 10.3

Read and write the following sentences:

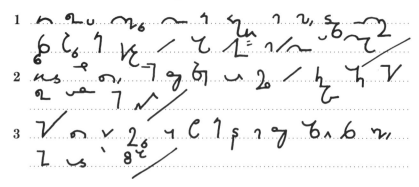

1

2

3

Dictation practice

Read the following passages and prepare for dictation.

1 Notice of meeting

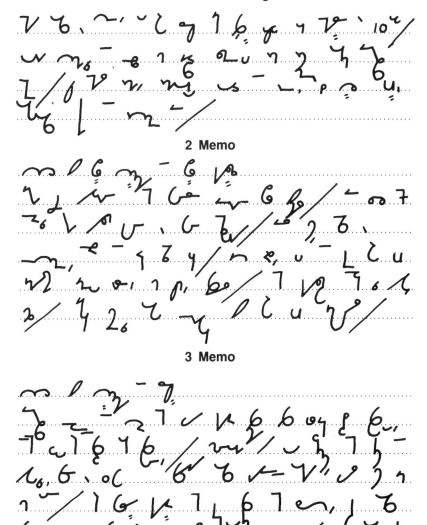

2 Memo

3 Memo

A disjoined vowel indicator with a **C** added gives us more word endings.

ANK: A indicator plus **C** … ᘓ ….

        ⁊ᘓ   ⟋ᘓ   oᘓ

    thank   rank   sank

Other letters may be added to the disjoined ending:

        ⁊ᘓ,   ⁊ᘓ   6ᘓ   ᘓᘓ
                           6

    thanking   thankless   banks   clanked

INK: I indicator plus **C** … ᘓ ….

     ⁊ᘓ   oᘓ   Iᘓ   ᘓᘓ   ᵞᘓ,   ⟋ᘓ

    think sink pink   *and* blinked shrinking wrinkle

ONK: O indicator plus **C** … ᘓ ….

     ⌒ᘓ   Iᘓ   cᘓ   _ᘓ   Iᘓ

    monk   honk   *and*   conker   donkey   honked

UNK: U indicator plus **C** … ᘓ ….

     oᘓ   Iᘓ   ᵞᘓ   ꟼᘓ

    sunk   hunk   shrunk   *and*   chunky

Exercise 11.1

Read and write the following sentences:

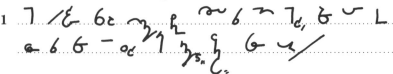

2

3

4

5

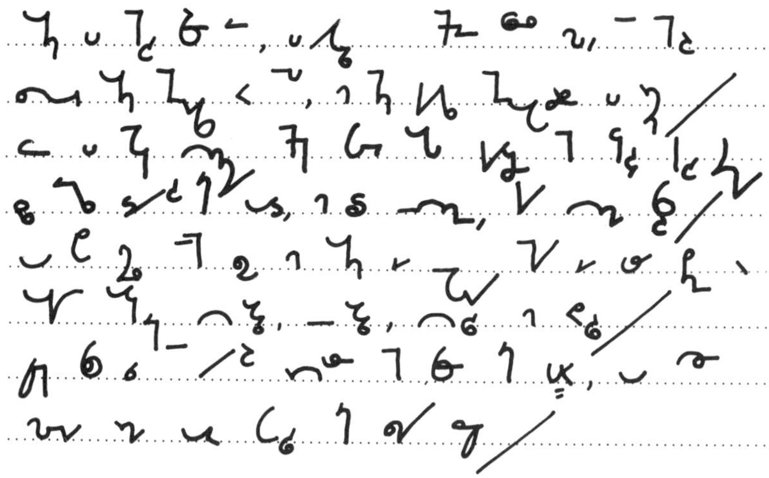

Special outlines

enclose   enclosed

Word groupings

I think    we think    thank you

we enclose    thank you for your letter

thank you for your enquiry    vote of thanks

thank you for your cheque

Exercise 11.2

Read and write the following sentences:

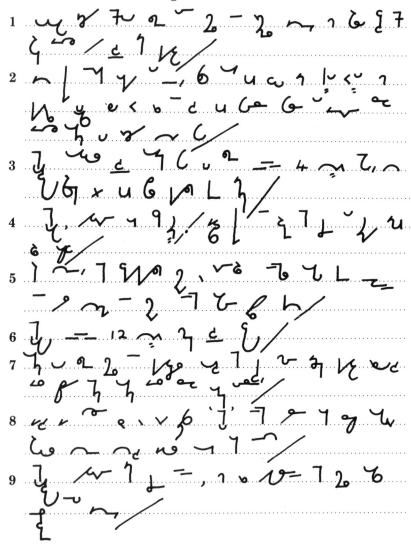

1

2

3

4

5

6

7

8

9

Dictation practice

Read the following passages and prepare for dictation.

1 Letter to a potential customer

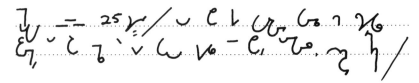

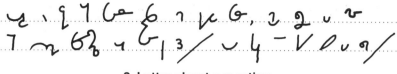

2 Letter about a meeting

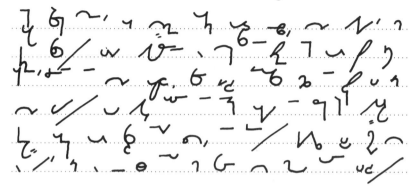

3 Extract from a talk on office duties

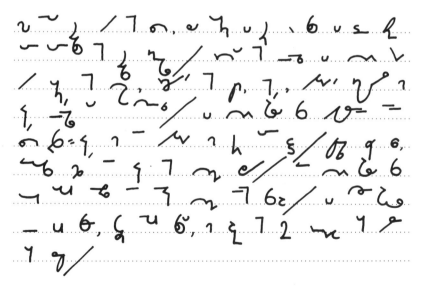

Word endings -NCE, -CH and -NCH

-NCE

A **C** disjoined at the end of a word represents the ending **-NCE** with any preceding vowel or combination of vowels.

⎺c	⟋⟍c	oc	*ℓc*
dance	distance	since	fence

Other letters can be added:

S ⌣₆	↑₆	*ℓ₆*
allowances	finances	balances

D *ℓc*	⟍c	*ℓc*
silenced	announced	balanced

R ⎺↙	⟍↙	*ℓ↙*
dancer	announcer	silencer

and the **-ING** ending

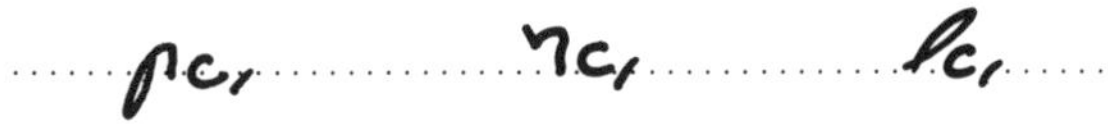

↑c₍	⟍c₍	*ℓc₍*
financing	announcing	fencing

By adding **Y** we have:

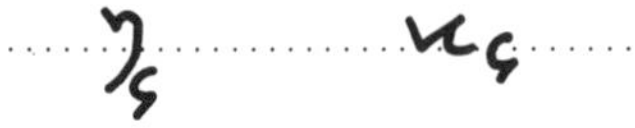

⟋ᵧ	⌐ᵧ
agency	vacancy

Exercise 12.1

Read and write the following sentences:

1 ᵎ ⎽ ⟍ ⟋⟍c *ℓ* ⌐ h ⊐ ↗ *ℓ* ᵎ/

2 ᵎ ⟍ ℔c 6 ⟋ 2 ⟍ *ℓ↙* ↗ ⌐ ↙ ₀

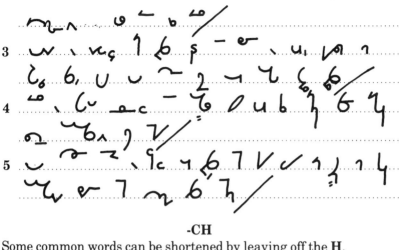

-CH

Some common words can be shortened by leaving off the **H**.

৬	ॡ	℮	u
each	much	such	which

Many other words like this will occur to you and they can be safely written in this way.

-NCH

A disjoined **CH** at the end of a word represents **-NCH**.

Cৎ	6ৎ	lৎ
lunch	bench	punch

Add other endings:

Cৎ	Cৎ,	lৎ
luncheon	lunching	punched

Exercise 12.2

Read and write the following sentences:

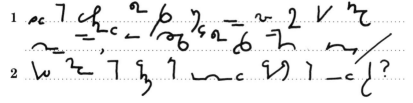

3

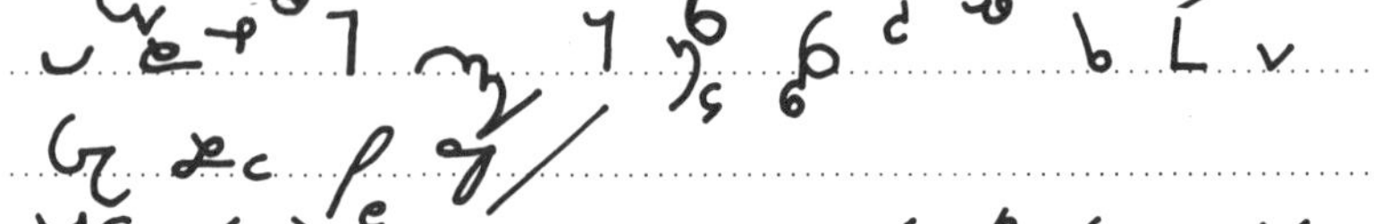

4

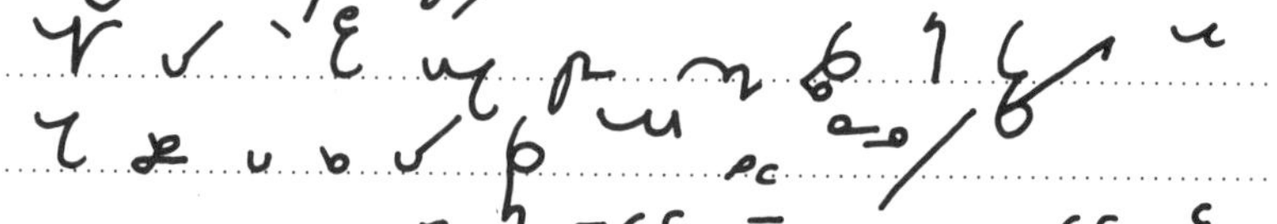

5

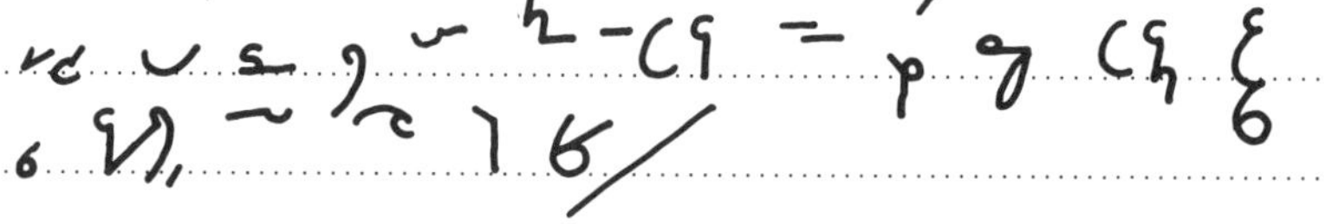

Special outlines

circumstance	circumstances	difference	different

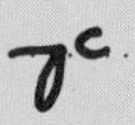

insurance	once

Word groupings

at once	in the circumstances	such things

each day	too much

Exercise 12.3

Read and write the following sentences:

1

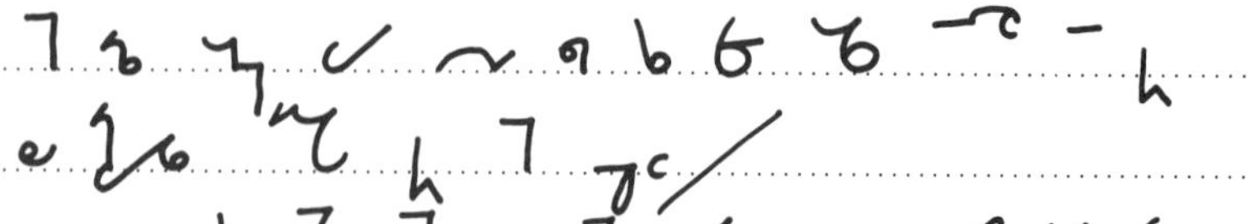

2

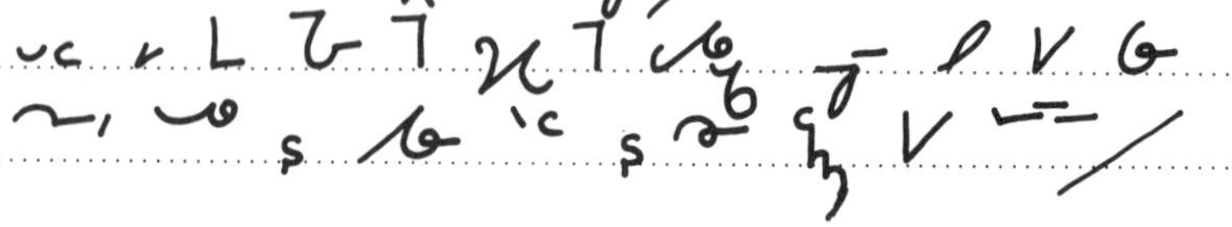

3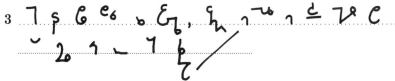

Dictation practice
Read the following passages and prepare for dictation.

1 Rebate on electricity account

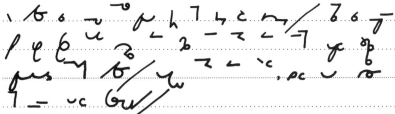

2 Hotel booking in Paris

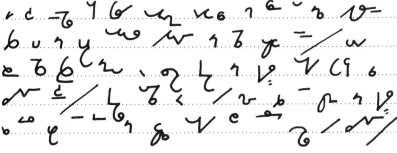

3 Sales meeting

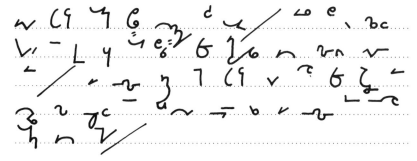

The letters **F** and **L** are special in Teeline because they have more than one form. This is to make the joining of letters clearer and easier.

Letter F

It can be written upwards .... or downwards ......

You will have a better outline if you use the downward **F** before

N:	C:	V:	K:
fine	face	five	fake

If you keep in mind **T** – **T**op, **D** – **D**own you will have no trouble when you write words such as:

food	foot	deaf	tough

In all these words the **T** and **D** keep to their proper places. With other letters choose whichever way of writing you find easier.

Letter L

This has three forms .... *or* .... *or* ....

.... is the one used in most cases.

lost	lip	cool	leave

.... By chopping off the bottom curl, you will get a better outline when the **L** is followed by

C:	G:	M:	N:	
luck	colleague	lamb	line	Teeline

⟨⟨ This is the upward **L** and should be regarded as a convenience letter to make neater outlines. It is only used at the end of a word or sometimes in the middle. It is *never* used at the beginning of a word. For instance, if **L** follows a letter which has cut the line, such as a **G**, **P** or **J**, the ordinary Teeline **L** would interfere with the next line of notes. In these cases, use an upward **L**.

For example: ⟨⟩ pills looks far better than ⟨⟩.

The outlines ⟨⟩ glass ⟨⟩ pulling ⟨⟩ jail all look better when written with an upward **L**.

You can also use the upward **L** after

H: ⟨⟩ **M:** ⟨⟩ **N:** ⟨⟩

   help   small   nail

However, if you have used the upward **L**, the **I** indicator must also be written upward as in:

⟨⟩ ⟨⟩ ⟨⟩

 hilly   Millie   jelly

Exercise 13.1

Read and write the following sentences:

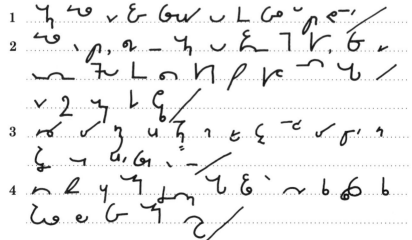

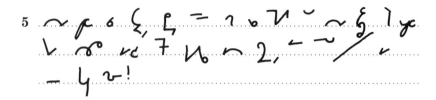

T and D after R and upward L

Always disjoin the letters **T** and **D** when they follow an **R** or an
upward **L**. This gives a better and more recognisable outline.

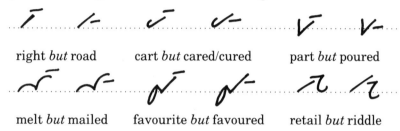

right *but* road   cart *but* cared/cured   part *but* poured

melt *but* mailed   favourite *but* favoured   retail *but* riddle

Exercise 13.2

Read and write the following sentences:

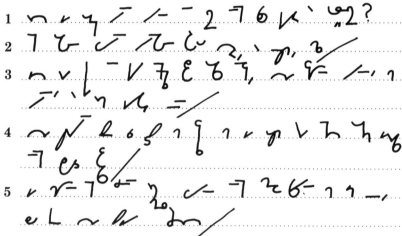

F blends

Many Teeline letters join more easily if they are blended, as we did
with **O** and **M** (Unit 9). When we do this it takes less time to write
than two letters and yet they can still be seen clearly in the one
outline. The letter **F** blends well with other letters because it has
two forms. When writing the **F** and **R** or **F** and **L** blends it makes no

difference whether the letters come together or if there is a vowel between.

F + R: .... *as in* .... for .... first .... Fred

R + F: .... *as in* .... rough .... surfing .... refuse

F + L: .... *as in* .... flying .... follow .... faulty

The **F** and **L** blend is useful at the end of a word when it can be written .... *or* ....

Look at these:

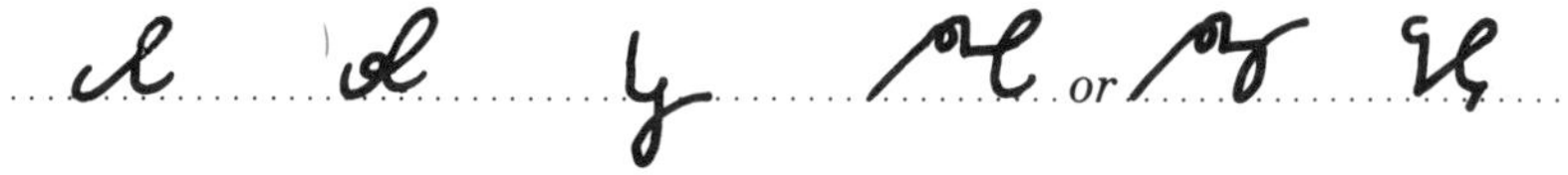

careful useful hopeful resentful cheerfully

The letter **F** can also be blended with several other letters and in some cases it means the **F** has to be put on its side.

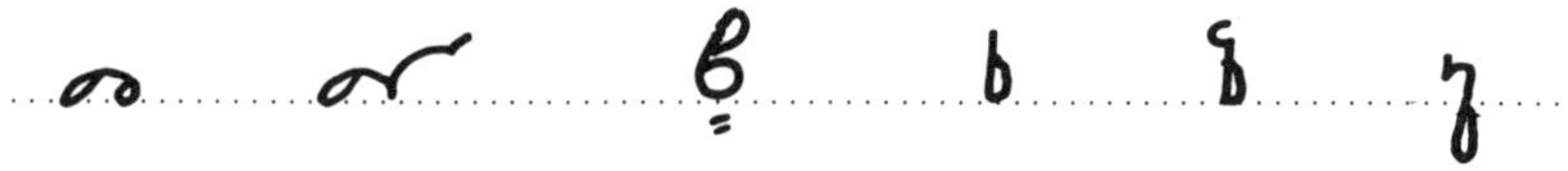

famous family February half chief enough

Exercise 13.3

Read and write the following sentences:

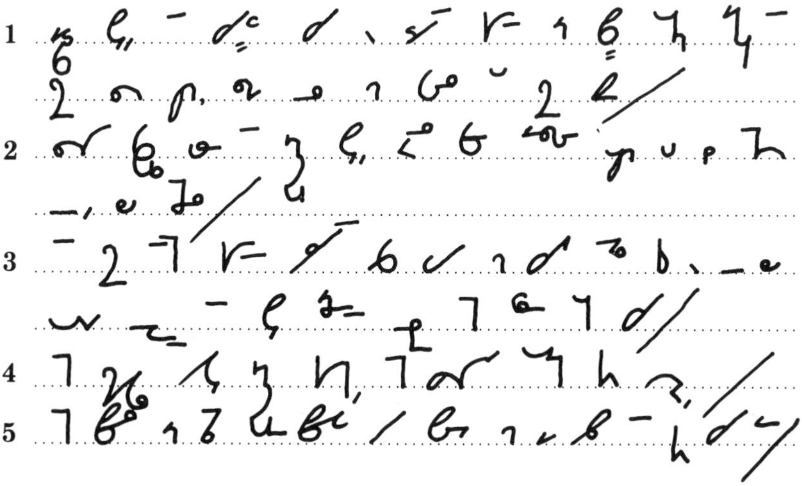

Special outlines

before   telephone   reference   satisfactory

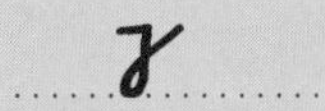

therefore

Distinguishing outlines

firm   form   farm

Word groupings

all sorts of things   first time   first class

referring to   with reference to

with reference to your letter   business letter

Exercise 13.4

Read and write the following sentences:

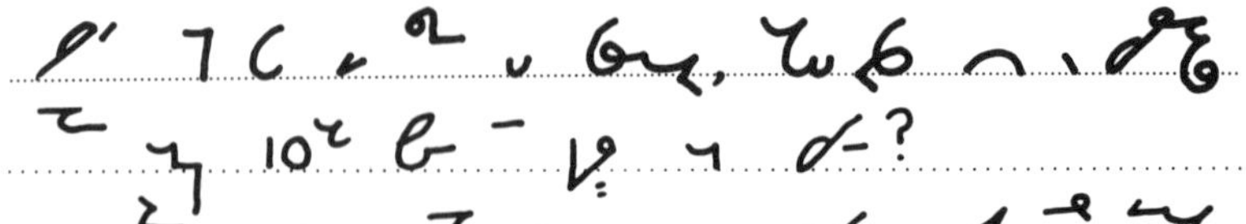

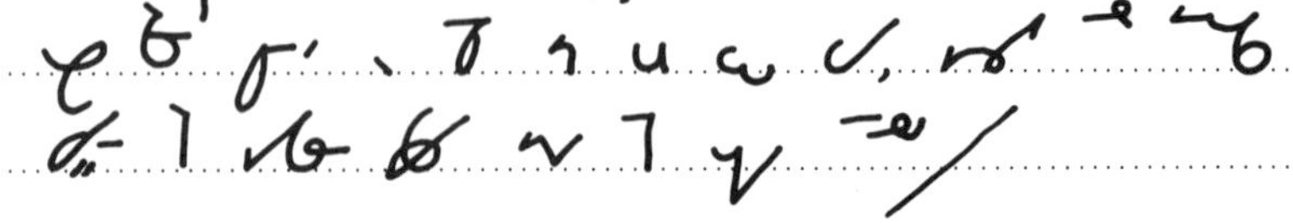

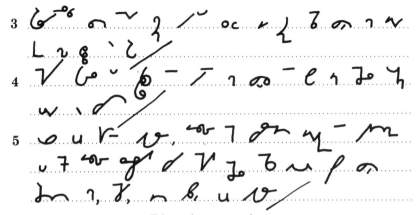

3

4

5

Dictation practice
Read the following passages and prepare for dictation.

1 Refuse collection from flats

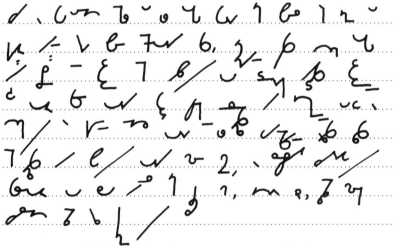

2 Why are business letters so boring?

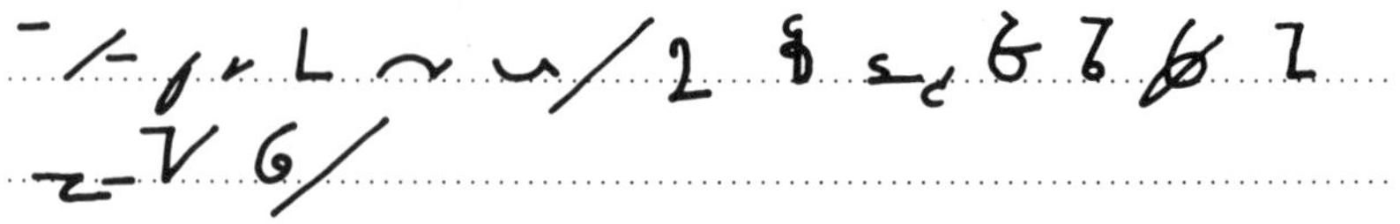

3 Problems of shared telephones

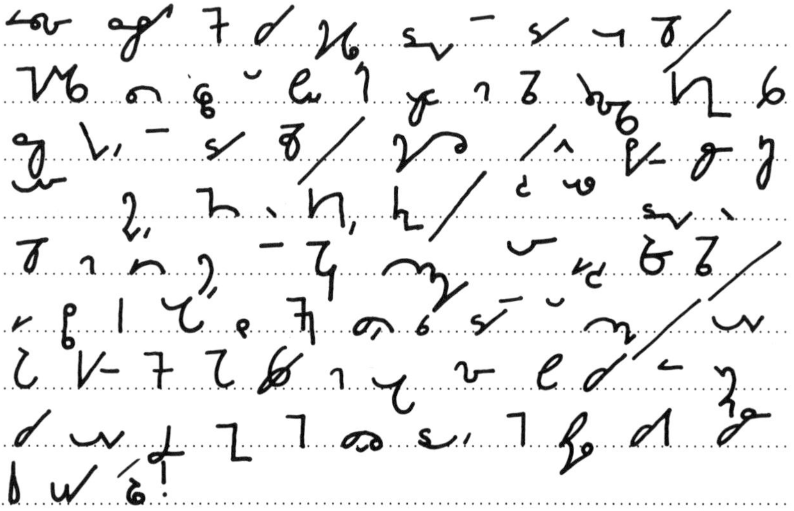

-MENT

This ending is written as a small disjoined **M** written in the **T** position close to the rest of the word.

appointment   payment   moment   document   management

The ending -**MENT** can be further extended by adding other letters:

-**MENTAL** ....   sentimental   fundamental

-**MENTALLY** ....   monumentally   temperamentally

-**MENTARY** ....   elementary   parliamentary

-**MENTS/ MENTALS** ....   elements   fundamentals

Special outlines

advertisement   department   government

requirement   amount   development

Word groupings

in fact   in favour   last time   last minute

Houses of Parliament   Member of Parliament

Exercise 14.1

Read and write the following sentences:

1

2

3

4

5

-SELF

Write **SL** only, either upwards or downwards, whichever is more convenient.

| myself | yourself | himself | herself | itself | oneself |

-SELVES

Add an **S** to the **-SELF** ending.

| themselves | yourselves |

Exercise 14.2

Read and write the following sentences:

1

2

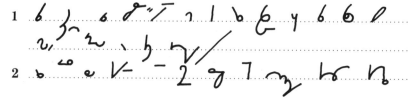

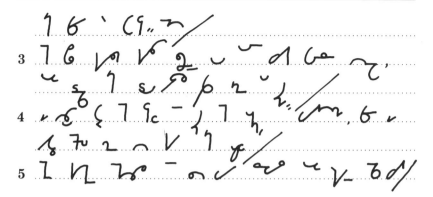

Dictation practice
Read the following passages and prepare for dictation.

1 Flight bookings

2 Daydreaming

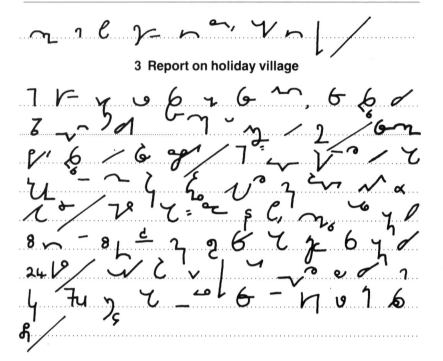

3 Report on holiday village

Unit 15
Word endings -SHUN, -SHL, -SHIP

-SHUN

A disjoined **N** written in the **T** position close to the previous part of
the outline represents **-TION** and the sound of **-SHUN**, however
this is spelt.

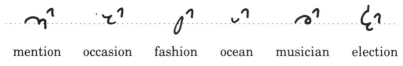

| mention | occasion | fashion | ocean | musician | election |

-SHUN may be extended by adding other letters.

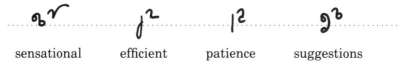

| sensational | efficient | patience | suggestions |

Words ending in **LY** may be shortened by omitting the **L**.

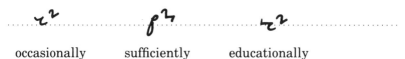

| occasionally | sufficiently | educationally |

Vowels may be added to the disjoined ending to make reading back
easier, although this is not usually necessary.

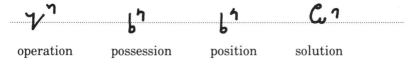

| operation | possession | position | solution |

Exercise 15.1

Read and write the following sentences:

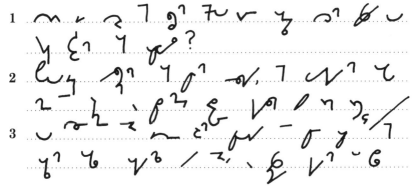

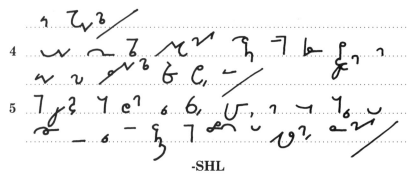

4

5

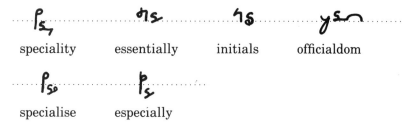

-SHL

Some word endings sound **-SHL** but can be spelt **-TIAL** or **-CIAL**.
In both cases a disjoined **SH** is used, written near to the end of the
previous stroke.

special   initial   essential   social   official

circumstantial

-SHL can be extended by adding other letters.

speciality   essentially   initials   officialdom

specialise   especially

-SHIP

A *joined* **SH** represents the word ending **-SHIP**.

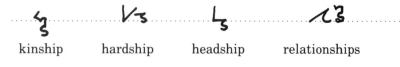

kinship   hardship   headship   relationships

Exercise 15.2

Read and write the following sentences:

1

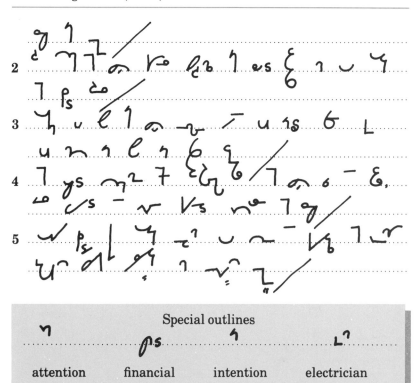

Special outlines

attention	financial	intention	electrician
particular	difficulty	manufacture	

Distinguishing outlines

specialist	specialised

Word groupings

your attention	immediate attention

Exercise 15.3

Read and write the following sentences:

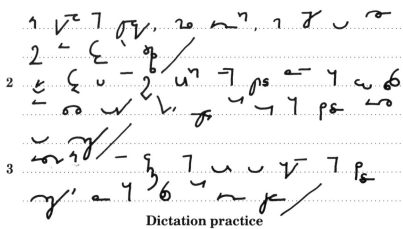

Dictation practice

Read the following passages and prepare for dictation.

1 Memo from machine shop manager to foreman

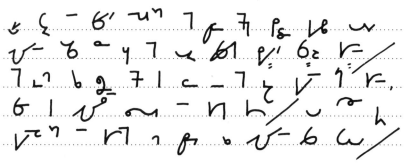

2 Letter to bank manager

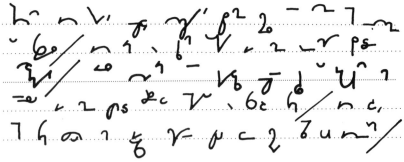

3 Memo from sales manager to sales staff

Unit 16
T and D blends

TR and DR
TR

When **T** and **R** occur next to each other, as well as when there is a
vowel in between them, the **T** and **R** strokes are blended together to
give one long stroke. The sign can be used anywhere in the outline
but it is written in the usual **T** position if it is the first stroke in a
word.

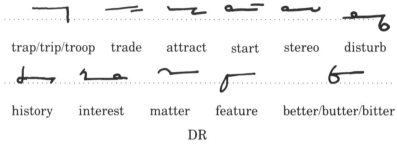

| trap/trip/troop | trade | attract | start | stereo | disturb |

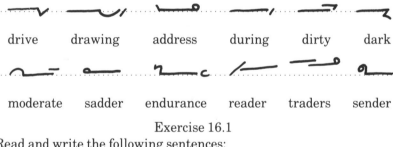

| history | interest | matter | feature | better/butter/bitter |

DR

Similarly, when **D** and **R** are written next to each other or with a
vowel between them blend them to give a lengthened **D** stroke
written in the **D** position at the beginning of an outline.

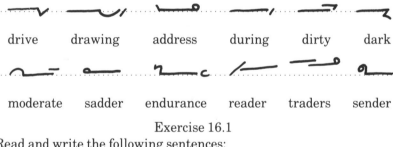

| drive | drawing | address | during | dirty | dark |

| moderate | sadder | endurance | reader | traders | sender |

Exercise 16.1

Read and write the following sentences:

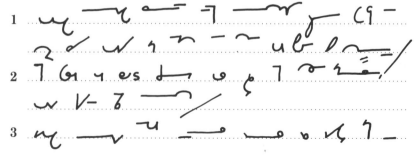

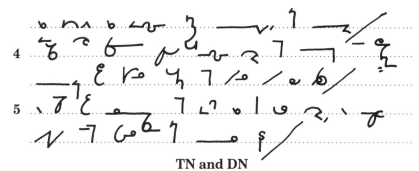

TN and DN

T and **D** can each be blended with **N**, by smoothing out the curve of the **N**.

TN

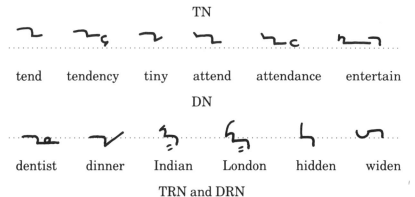

tend   tendency   tiny   attend   attendance   entertain

DN

dentist   dinner   Indian   London   hidden   widen

TRN and DRN

The double strokes of **TR** and **DR** can also be blended with **N**.

TRN

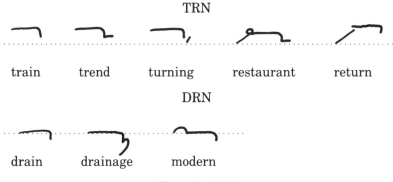

train   trend   turning   restaurant   return

DRN

drain   drainage   modern

Exercise 16.2

Read and write the following sentences:

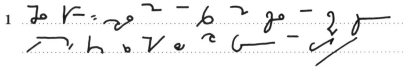

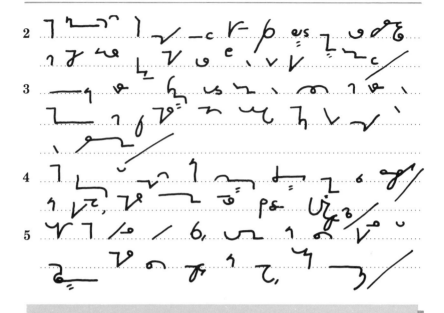

2
3
4
5

Special outline

yesterday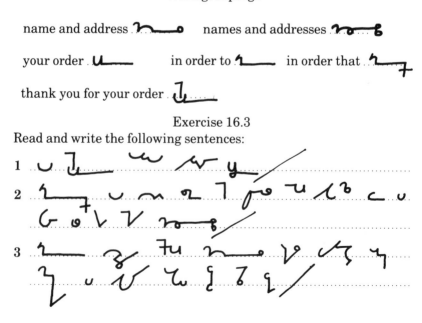

Word groupings

name and address   names and addresses

your order   in order to   in order that

thank you for your order

Exercise 16.3

Read and write the following sentences:

1
2
3

Dictation practice
Read the following passages and prepare for dictation.

1 Queen's Birthday Parade

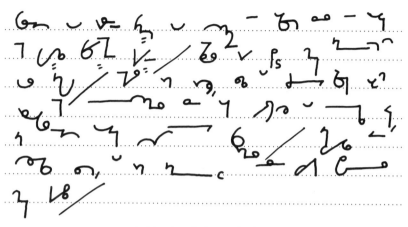

2 Traders' Association

3 Memo to tour operator

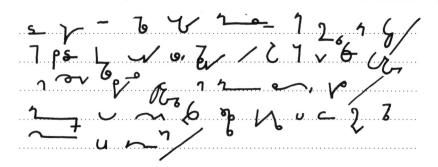

Unit 17
Business groupings

In business there are many groupings which are used frequently and practising these will increase your shorthand speed. Some very common groupings used in letter writing are:

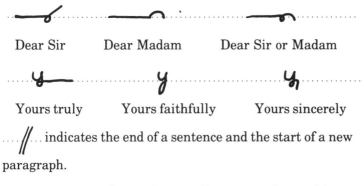

Dear Sir   Dear Madam   Dear Sir or Madam

Yours truly   Yours faithfully   Yours sincerely

.....//... indicates the end of a sentence and the start of a new paragraph.

..⁓. written underneath an outline means the word is

transcribed in full, eg .⌐. Wednesday.

You can now write a complete letter in Teeline. Read the following letters and then prepare them for dictation.

Exercise 17.1

Letter about damaged goods

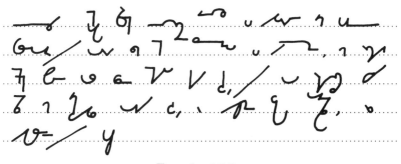

Exercise 17.2

Letter about a job application

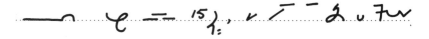

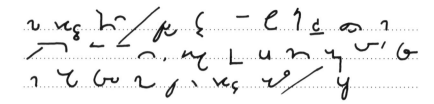

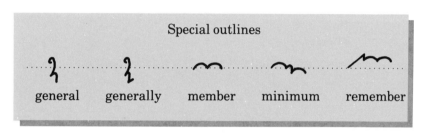

Special outlines

general	generally	member	minimum	remember

Exercise 17.3

Read and write the following sentences:

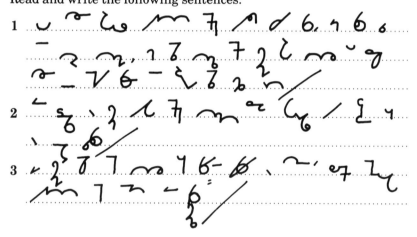

Dictation practice

Below are some more letters for you to read and practise.

1 Letter about an Annual General Meeting

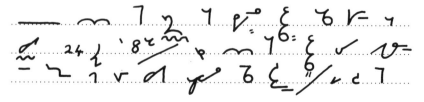

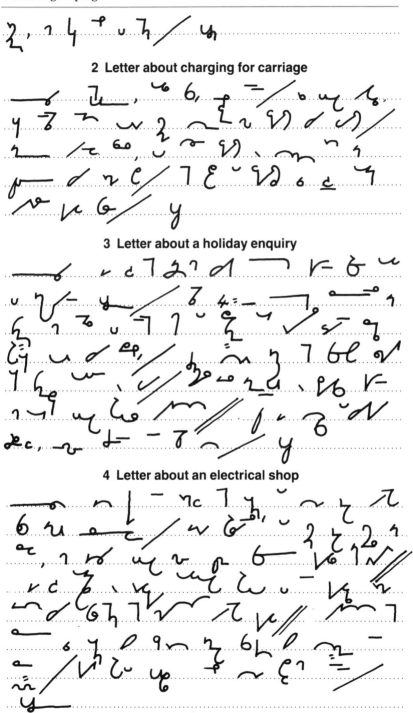

2 Letter about charging for carriage

3 Letter about a holiday enquiry

4 Letter about an electrical shop

Unit 18
Blends: THR, CTR, RN;
G or J and -NESS

The THR blend

The **TR** blend (see Unit 16) can also be used to show the sound of **THR** when it comes in the middle or at the end of a word. *Never* use it at the beginning of a word. So we could have:

other	rather	either	whether	gathering

smothered

But

thread	through	throwing

The **THR** blend can also be used for the words **there/their** in word groupings, but the same rule applies – it must only be used in the middle or at the end of the grouping.

.... is there   *but* .... there is

.... has there been   *but* .... there has been

Exercise 18.1

Read and write the following sentences:

1

2

3

4

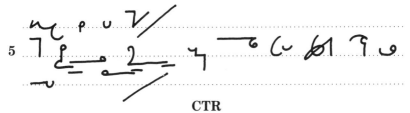

5

CTR

As we joined the **C** to **T** and **D** by lengthening the **C**; this principle can be extended to **CTR**.

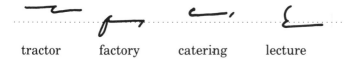

tractor   factory   catering   lecture

Be careful with words such as:

lecturer *and* caterer

where the final **R** must be shown.

RN blend

When writing **RN**, blend the two letters together so that they make

a smooth, continuous line . Make sure the straight stem of

the **N** points towards the writing line.

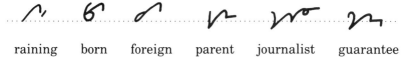

raining   born   foreign   parent   journalist   guarantee

Exercise 18.2

Read and write the following sentences:

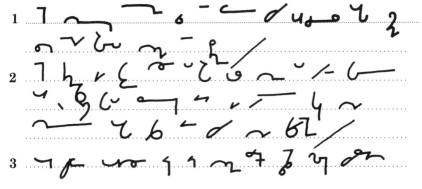

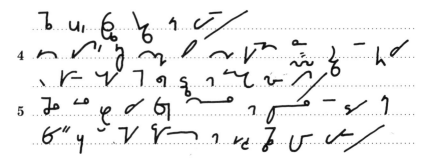

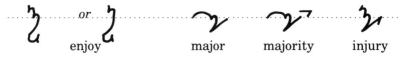

Letters G or J

After **M** and **N** it is sometimes easier to write the letter **G** instead of
J because it gives a clearer outline.

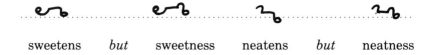

| enjoy | major | majority | injury |

-NESS

When a word ends with a strongly sounded **-NESS**, it should be
clear from the context whether, for example, the word is, *sweetens*
or *sweetness*, but to help you transcribe quickly and accurately it is

safe to show the difference so use ⟨ symbol ⟩ for **-NESS**.

| sweetens | *but* | sweetness | neatens | *but* | neatness |

Exercise 18.3

Read and write the following sentences:

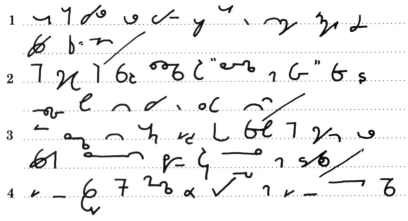

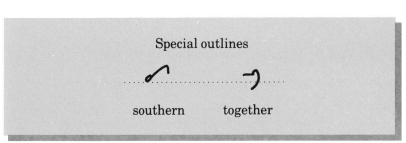

Special outlines

southern   together

Distinguishing outlines

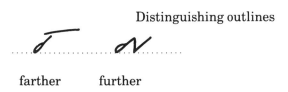

farther   further

Word groupings

during their   ,   that there/their   be there/their

some other   on the other hand

Exercise 18.4
Read and write the following sentences:

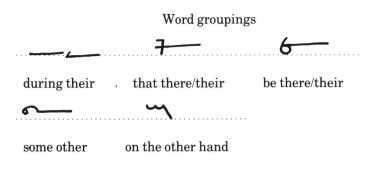

4

Dictation practice
Read the following passages and prepare for dictation.

1 Waiting for hospital appointments

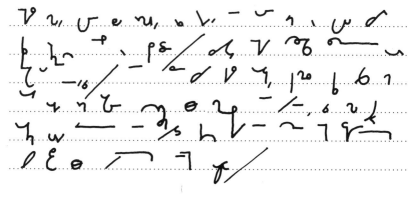

2 Down Memory Lane

3 Letter cancelling a meeting

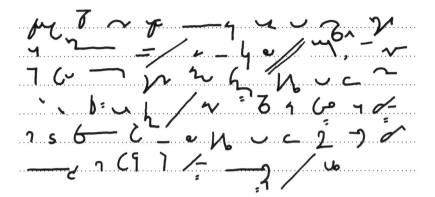

Unit 19
Blends: LR, MR, WR and WK, WRK

Lengthened strokes

As well as **T** and **D**, three other letters are lengthened to add **R**: **L**, **M** and **W**. In each case, there is usually a vowel between **L**, **M**, **W** and the **R**.

LR

This is generally written downwards, but after some strokes can be written upwards to give a better outline.

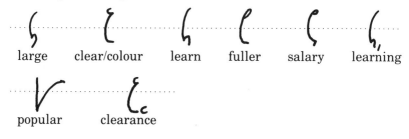

large	clear/colour	learn	fuller	salary	learning

popular	clearance

Exercise 19.1

Read and write the following sentences:

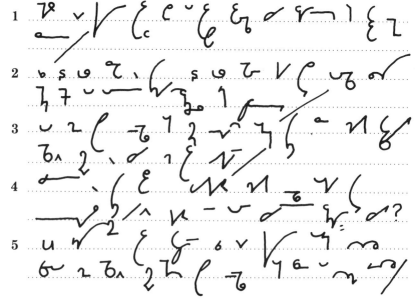

MR

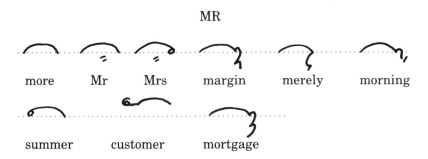

more	Mr	Mrs	margin	merely	morning

summer	customer	mortgage

Exercise 19.2

Read and write the following sentences:

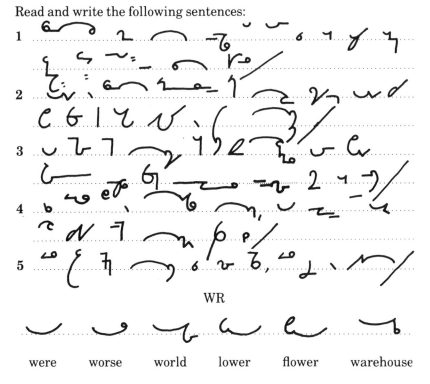

WR

were	worse	world	lower	flower	warehouse

WK and WRK blends
WK

When joining **W** to **K**, the first stroke of **K** is written backwards along **W**, so that only the second stroke of **K** is shown.

week/weak	weekend	walking

WRK

WR and **K** may be joined by using the long **WR** stroke and adding **K** in the same way.

work   workman   workshop

When joining **R** or **D** to **WK** or **WRK**, it is easier to write **C** than **K**.

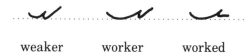

weaker   worker   worked

Exercise 19.3

Read and write the following sentences:

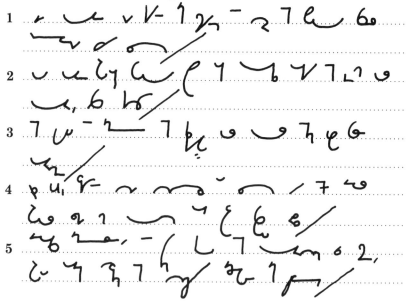

NB: it's important to keep the difference in size – *check your outlines.*

ment	⌒	would/word/etc	◡
M	⌒	W	◡
MR	⌢	WR	◡

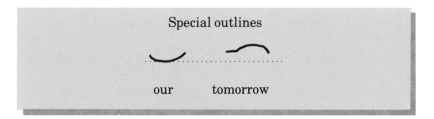

Special outlines

our   tomorrow

Distinguishing outlines

were   where

Word groupings

worthwhile   this morning

more and more   more or less   more than

smaller and smaller   larger and larger

Dear Mr   Dear Mrs   Dear Miss   Dear Ms

sum of money   sums of money

parts of the world   all parts of the world

Exercise 19.4

Read and write the following sentences:

1

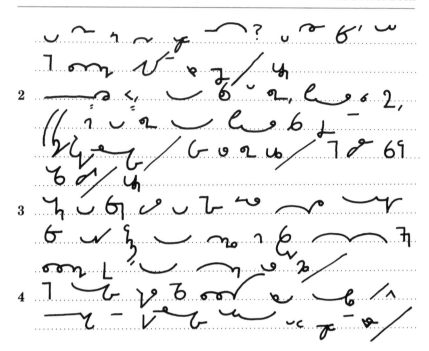

Dictation practice
Read the following passages and prepare for dictation.

1 Letter about a repair to a tap

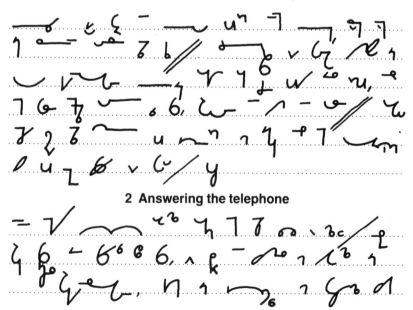

2 Answering the telephone

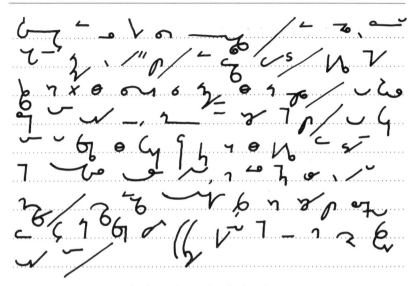

3 Opening a florist's shop

Unit 20
Numbers, currencies and colloquialisms

Numbers

Numbers 1–99 can be written as figures. To avoid the danger of misreading 1 as **he**, 6 as **be** and 7 as **the**, these numbers should be ringed when standing alone:

Hundred: use the **DR** blend, written under the number of hundreds.

300

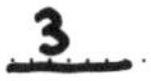

Thousand: use the **THS** sign to enclose the figures.

3000

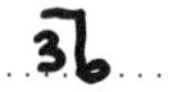

Hundred thousand: use a blend of **DR** and **THS** under the figures.

300 000

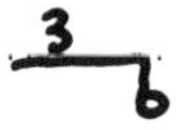

Million: use **M** written under the figure.

3 000 000

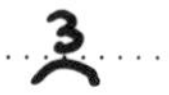

Hundred million: use a combination of **DR** and **M** under the figure.

3 hundred million

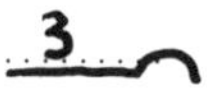

Thousand million: use **THS** and **M** round the figure.

3 thousand million

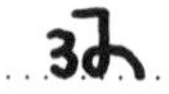

If the words hundred, thousand and million are used without a figure, the whole word should be written in full.

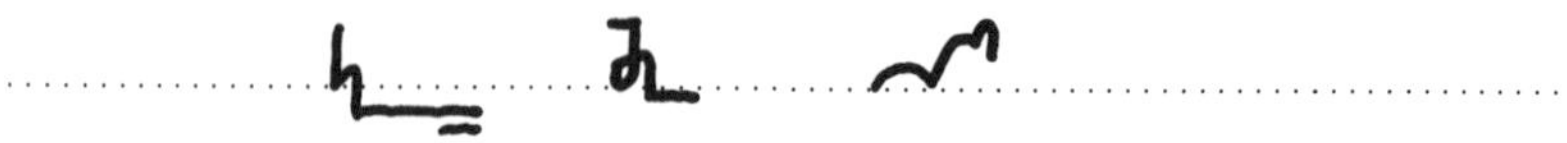

Exercise 20.1

Read and write the following sentences:

1

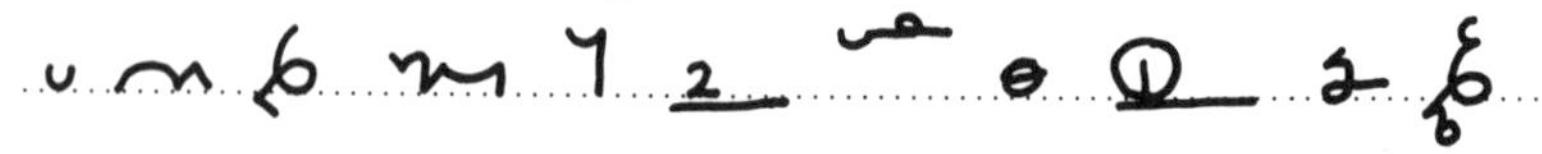

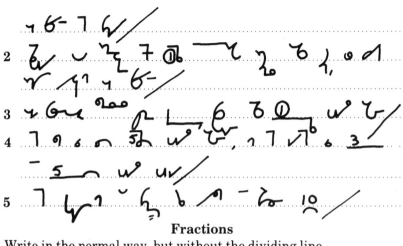

Fractions

Write in the normal way, but without the dividing line.

2/3 $\frac{2}{3}$ 9/16 $\frac{9}{16}$

Per cent

Use the Teeline letters **P** and **R** after the figure.

8 per cent   1 per cent   100%

Per cent per annum

Write two **P**s after the figure.

4½ per cent per annum   10 per cent per annum

Currencies

Pounds: use **PDS** *after* the figure, so that the speed of writing is not slowed down.

£6   £600   £6000

Dollars: use **DS** under the figure.

$6 $600 $6 million

Deutschmark: use **DM** after the figures.

15 DM   5000 DM

Franc: use **F** after the figures.

34 F ...**34 /**....   7 million francs ..**7 /**....

Dates
In dates beginning with 19, only the last two digits need to be
written.

1992 ....**92**.....   1928 ...**28**......   *but* 1892

Century
Rather than write out the word century, put a large **C** in front of the
figure.

20th century ..**⟨20**....   17th century ...**⟨17**....

Exercise 20.2

Read and write the following sentences:

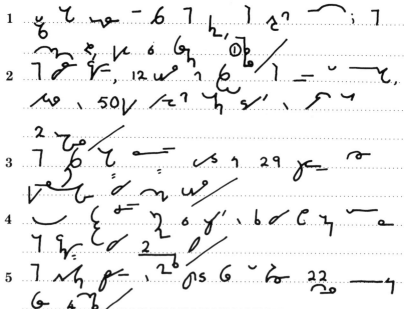

Colloquial forms of speech
If it is necessary to show contractions (words like I'm and don't),
then an apostrophe is placed above the outline:

I'm ...✦... *but* I am ...⌒... he's ...**ᑅ**... *but* he is ...**ᑊ**...

Special outlines

ว .... ໃ

number   number of

Exercise 20.3

Read and write the following sentences:

1

2

3

4

5

Dictation practice

Read the following passages and prepare for dictation.

1 The holiday market

2 Tourism in France

3 French skiing holidays

Unit 21
X blends

Letter X

The letter **X** blends well with many letters simply by writing one of the **X** strokes (usually ❭) and crossing it with the following letter.

When a word begins with **EX** there is no need to write the **E** – it can be heard in the sound of the **X** and this is sufficient. Here are some examples of **X** blend words:

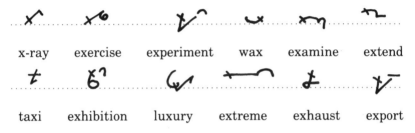

x-ray	exercise	experiment	wax	examine	extend

taxi	exhibition	luxury	extreme	exhaust	export

NB: in the word 'exist' the **X** should be written in full

Exercise 21.1
Read and write the following sentences:

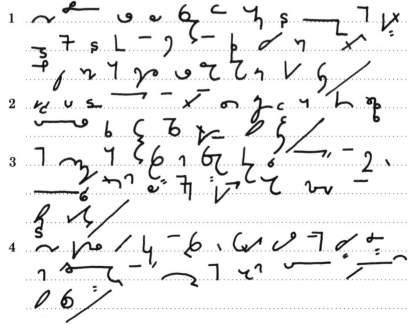

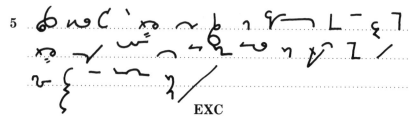

5

EXC

Some words start with **EXC**. As we left out the **E** in words like
'export', so we can leave out the **C** if it too is included in the **X**
sound.

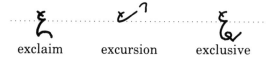

excellent   excellence   excerpt

If the C does have a definite sound it must be shown as in:

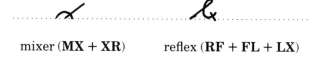

exclaim   excursion   exclusive

Sometimes when blending **X** with other letters you may have more
than one blend:

mixer (**MX + XR**)   reflex (**RF + FL + LX**)

NX blend

Put the **N** on its side so that it forms the first stroke of the **X**.

or

next   annexe   inexpensive

Exercise 21.2

Read and write the following sentences:

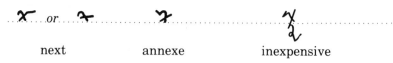

1

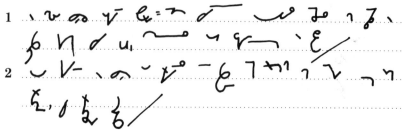

2

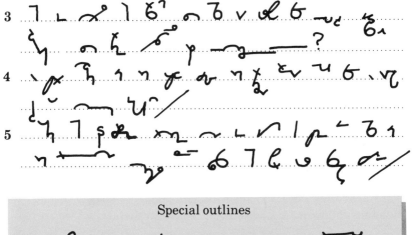

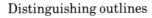

Special outlines

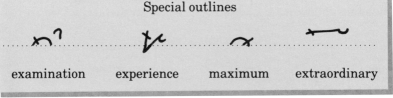

| examination | experience | maximum | extraordinary |

Distinguishing outlines

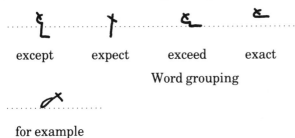

| except | expect | exceed | exact |

Word grouping

for example

Exercise 21.3

Read and write the following sentences:

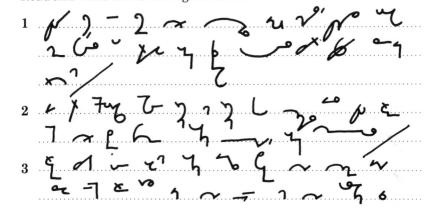

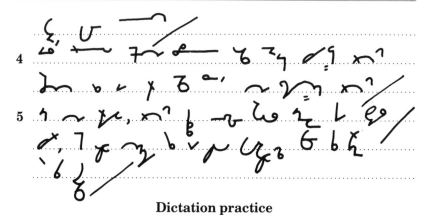

Dictation practice

Read the following passages and prepare for dictation.

1 A visit to the dentist

2 Foreign currency exchange rate

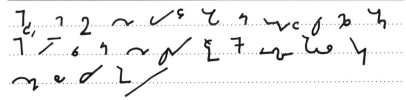

3 Noticeboard announcement of sponsored walk

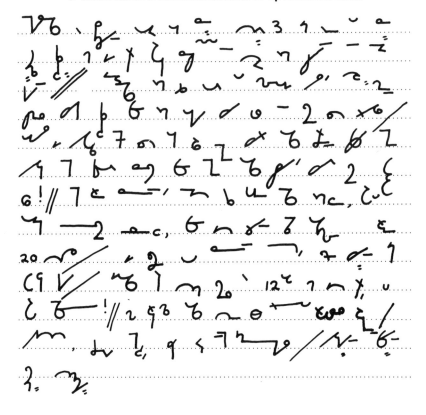

C vowel **M** is represented in Teeline by a blend of **C** and **M**. The shallow **C** shape is written as wide as the **M**, but twice the length of **C**, so it shows the characteristics of both letters. Any vowel can occur between **C** and **M**, and the sound may be hard or soft.

⌐... can be used anywhere in the outline.

campaign	common	computer	committee

chemist	welcome	cement

Circle **S** can be written inside the **CM** blend as in:

scheme	scampi

ACCOM

⌐... Write indicator **A** before **CM**

accommodate	accommodation	accompany

UNACCOM

⌐..... **UN** is represented by indicator **U** immediately

before **ACCOM**

unaccompanied

ENCOM/INCOM/UNCOM

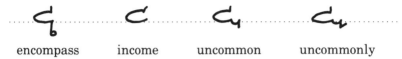 Omit **N** and join **E, I** or **U** indicator to **CM** to avoid an

awkward outline.

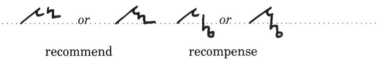

encompass   income   uncommon   uncommonly

RECOM

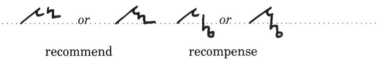 This prefix does not use the **CM** blend, but is reduced to

RC, which may be joined or disjoined from the rest of the word:

recommend   recompense

Exercise 22.1

Read and write the following sentences:

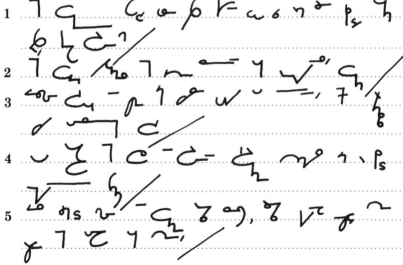

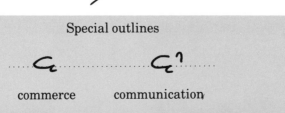

Special outlines

commerce   communication

Distinguishing outlines

If it is not obvious from the context, a safer distinction may be made by inserting vowel indicators:

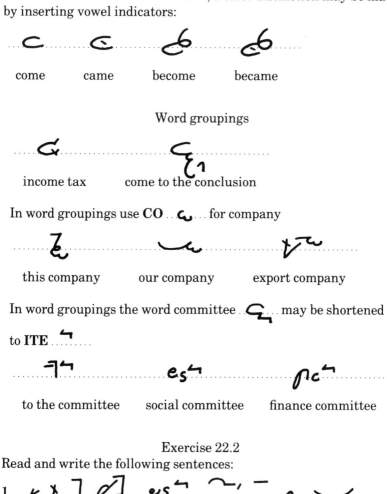

come   came   become   became

Word groupings

income tax   come to the conclusion

In word groupings use **CO** ⌣ for company

this company   our company   export company

In word groupings the word committee ⌣ may be shortened

to **ITE** ⌐

to the committee   social committee   finance committee

Exercise 22.2

Read and write the following sentences:

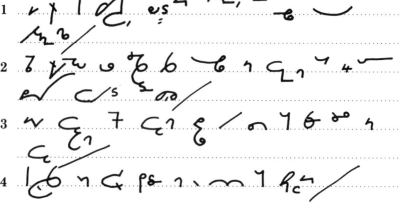

1

2

3

4

5

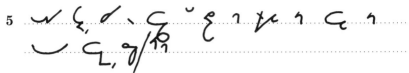

Dictation practice

Read the following passages and prepare for dictation.

1 The English seaside

2 Tourism survey

[shorthand notation]

3 Classification of accommodation

[shorthand notation]

Unit 23
N and V blends, NW and WN, words beginning EV

N and V

In order to make simpler outlines, **N** and **V** can be blended together or with other letters. Any vowel sound can occur between the two blended letters.

NV

N is sloped to form the first part of the **V**.

November	invoice	novice	envy	navy

VN

N is blended with the second stroke of the **V**, the **N** stroke ending on the writing line.

van	advantage	venue	vinyl	veneer	inventory

VR

R is added, lengthening the second stroke of **V**.

vary	reverse	severely	vertical	verdict

Exercise 23.1

Read and write the following sentences:

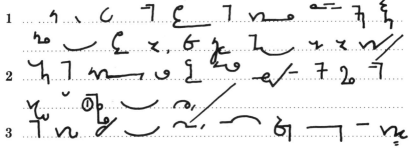

1

2

3

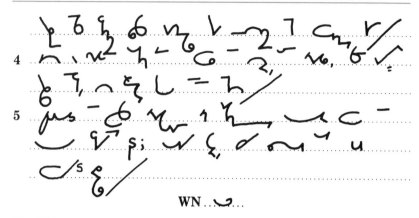

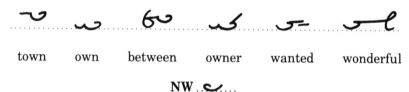

WN

The **N** is turned on its side and written inside the **W** curve:

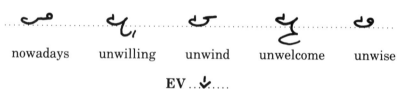

| town | own | between | owner | wanted | wonderful |

NW

Here again, the **N** is turned on its side and blended inside the **W** curve. For words starting **UNW** the **U** indicator is written

first

| nowadays | unwilling | unwind | unwelcome | unwise |

EV

Words beginning **EV** should be written with a disjoined **E** indicator above the **V**.

| evolve | evidence | evening | event | eventful | eventually |

EVER/EVERY

Words beginning with **EVER/EVERY** are also abbreviated to

| ever | everything | everyone | everywhere | everybody |

Words ending in **-EVER** are written with a disjoined **V** beneath the previous part of the outline:

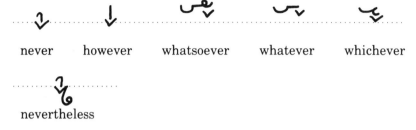

never   however   whatsoever   whatever   whichever

nevertheless

Exercise 23.2

Read and write the following sentences:

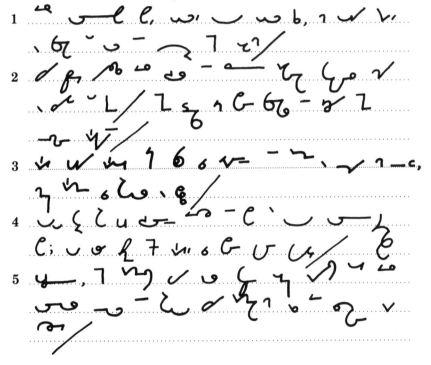

Special outline

several

Distinguishing outlines

lovely	lively	now	new/knew	know

Word groupings

in our view	in our opinion	in your company

no doubt	upside down

Exercise 23.3

Read and write the following sentences:

1

2

3

4

Dictation practice

Read the following passages and then prepare for dictation.

1 Letter of complaint

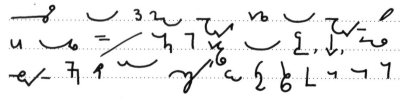

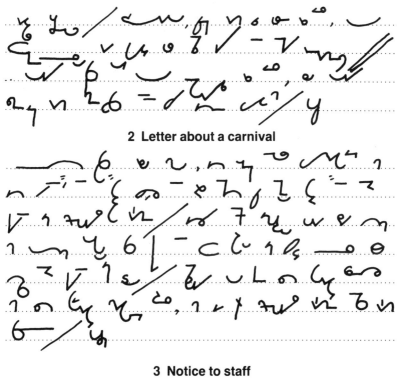

2 Letter about a carnival

3 Notice to staff

Unit 24
CN blends, INS

C–N

This blend is formed by using a reversed **N**, so that it begins with the **C** stroke. It represents **C** vowel **N**, using either a hard or soft sound **C**, just as we use a **C** in longhand.

can	contain	concentrate	central	economy

SC-N

Write the **S** circle inside the blend

scandal	scant

C-N and V-R

Slope the **CN** to form the first part of **V**.

canvas	converse	conversation

C-N and V-N

convene	convention	conventional

Exercise 24.1

Read and write the following sentences:

1

2

3

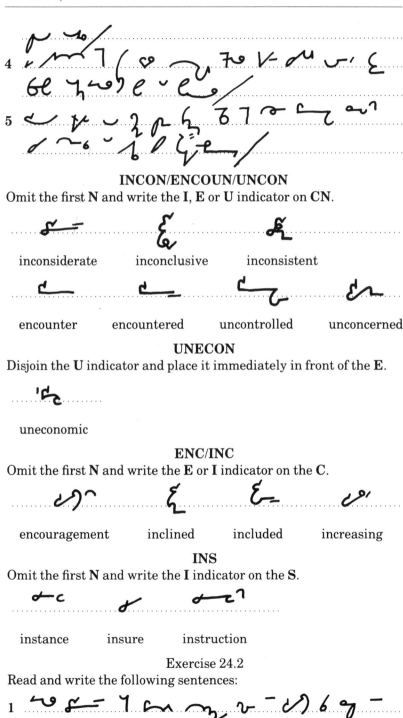

INCON/ENCOUN/UNCON

Omit the first **N** and write the **I**, **E** or **U** indicator on **CN**.

inconsiderate   inconclusive   inconsistent

encounter   encountered   uncontrolled   unconcerned

UNECON

Disjoin the **U** indicator and place it immediately in front of the **E**.

uneconomic

ENC/INC

Omit the first **N** and write the **E** or **I** indicator on the **C**.

encouragement   inclined   included   increasing

INS

Omit the first **N** and write the **I** indicator on the **S**.

instance   insure   instruction

Exercise 24.2

Read and write the following sentences:

1

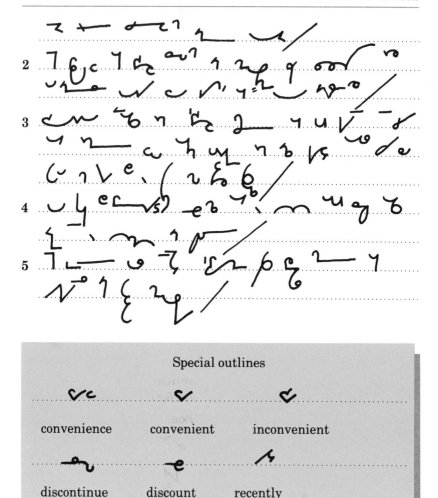

Special outlines

convenience   convenient   inconvenient

discontinue   discount   recently

Distinguishing outlines

cannot   can't   century   or   country

Word groupings

I can   can you   we can   for instance

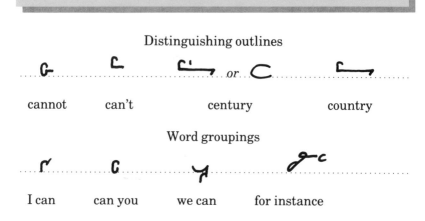

Exercise 24.3

Read and write the following sentences:

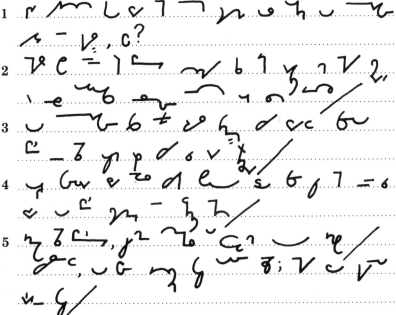

1

2

3

4

5

Dictation practice

Read the following passages and prepare for dictation.

1 Jury Service

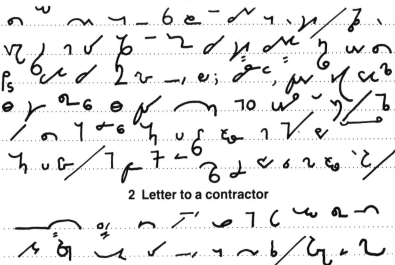

2 Letter to a contractor

3 Charity shops

Unit 25
P blends

P and V

The **P** is sloped and thus becomes the first stroke of **V**:

| pave | pavement | poverty |

P and L

When **P** and **L** occur together without a vowel between, *at the beginning of a word*, **L** is written in the **P** position, ie through the writing line.

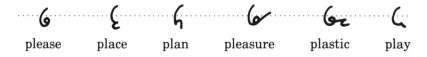

| please | place | plan | pleasure | plastic | play |

An initial vowel or an **S** can be added:

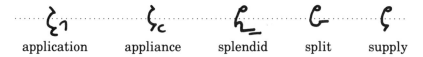

| application | appliance | splendid | split | supply |

But in the middle or at the end of a word, **PL** is written through the preceding consonant:

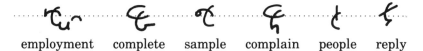

| employment | complete | sample | complain | people | reply |

However, where a vowel occurs between **P** and **L** (as in pill and compulsory), the **P** and the **L** must both be written.

Word groupings
PL can also represent the word people *in groupings*:

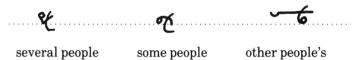

| several people | some people | other people's |

Exercise 25.1

Read and write the following sentences:

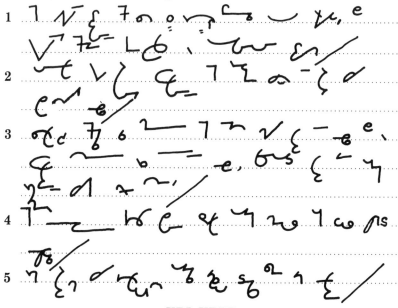

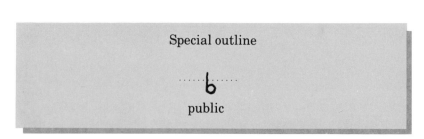

XPL/XPLR

Write the first stroke of **X** and then blend **PL** with it; or blend a lengthened **PL** to include **R**.

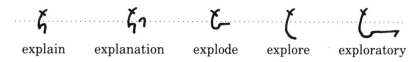

| explain | explanation | explode | explore | exploratory |

Special outline

$\flat$

public

Note that **P** and **B** are blended together.

From this same root we get words such as:

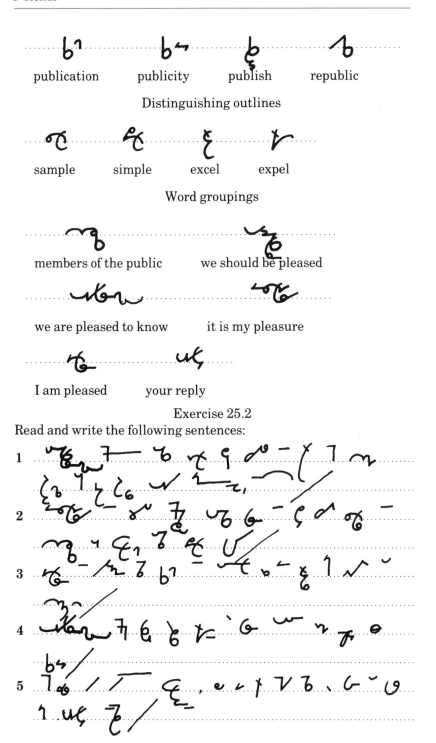

publication   publicity   publish   republic

Distinguishing outlines

sample   simple   excel   expel

Word groupings

members of the public   we should be pleased

we are pleased to know   it is my pleasure

I am pleased   your reply

Exercise 25.2

Read and write the following sentences:

1

2

3

4

5

Dictation practice
Read the following passages and prepare for dictation.

1 Reply to customer request

[shorthand]

2 Opening hours in public houses

[shorthand]

3 New public toilet

[shorthand]

Unit 26
Word beginnings – UNDER and ELECTRO

UNDER-

In order to avoid confusion with 'enter', **UNDER**, either as a word or a word-beginning, is written with a full **U** and with the **N** omitted

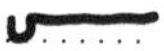

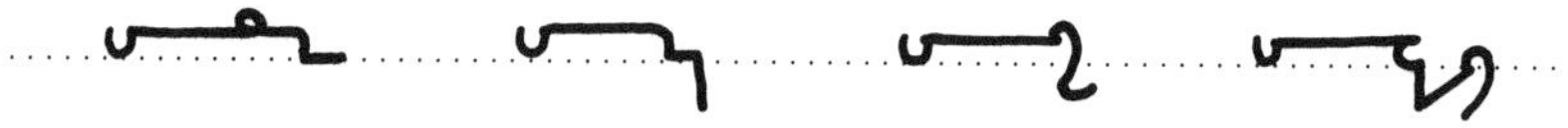

understand underneath undergo undercharge

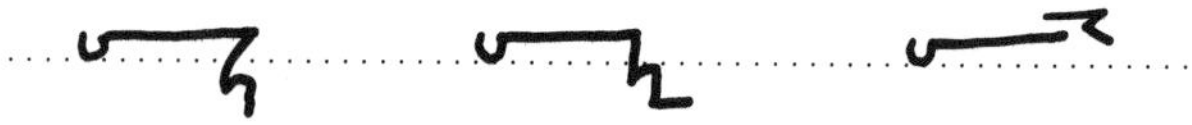

underline underhand undertake

ELECTRO-

As well as representing **ELECTRIC**, a disjoined full **E** is used for words beginning with **ELECTRO/ELECTRI**:

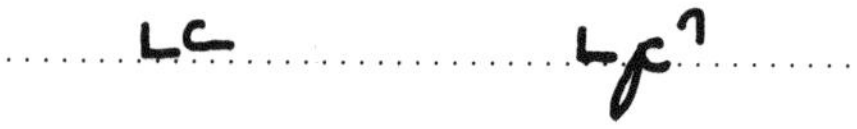

electrocute electrification

Special outline

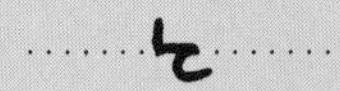

electronic

Word grouping

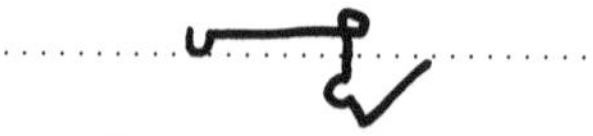

under separate cover

Exercise 26.1

Read the following sentences:

1

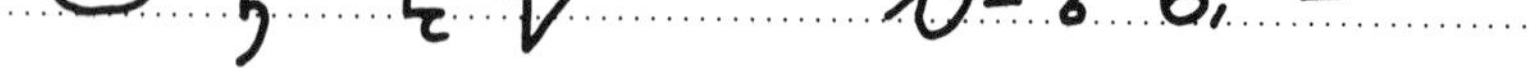

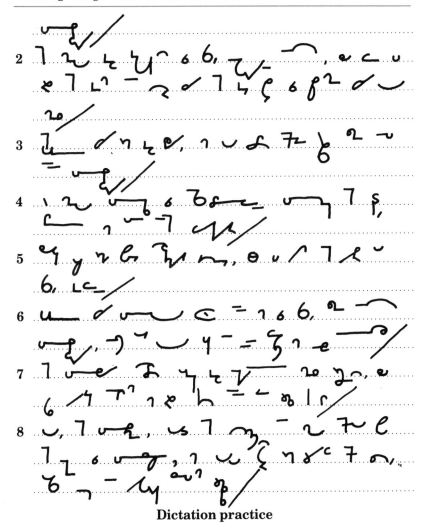

Dictation practice

Read the following passages and prepare for dictation.

1 Letter to a hotel about conference facilities

2 **Extract from Chairperson's Report**

3 **Letter about laying carpet**

Unit 27
Word beginnings – TRANS and OVER

TRANS-
This can be shortened to **TRS** by omitting the **N**.

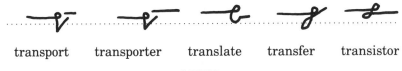

transport   transporter   translate   transfer   transistor

OVER
The **O** indicator is written *over* the rest of the outline.

overtake   overseas   overlook   overheads   overdue

NB: the word 'over' standing alone is written in full

Exercise 27.1
Read the following sentences:

1

2

3

4

5

Word groupings

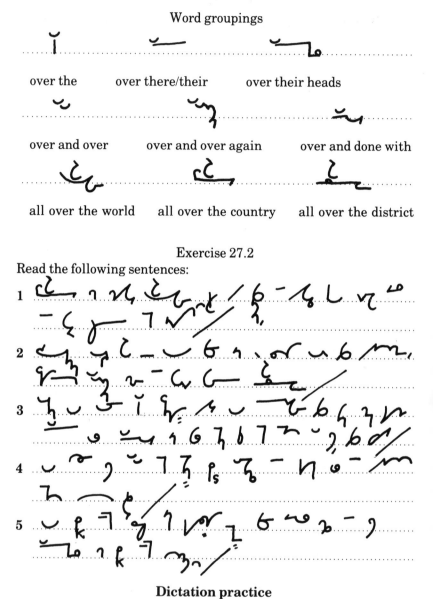

over the   over there/their   over their heads

over and over   over and over again   over and done with

all over the world   all over the country   all over the district

Exercise 27.2

Read the following sentences:

Dictation practice

Read the following passages and prepare for dictation.

1 Overdrawn account

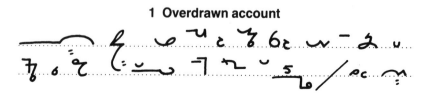

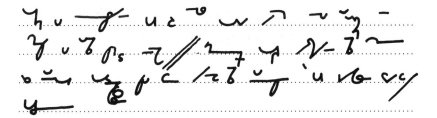

2 Appointment as courier

3 Extract from Company Report

Unit 28
Word beginnings – MULTI, NATION/NON, SEMI and SUPER

These are more useful abbreviated word beginnings which are in daily use.

MULTI
A disjoined **M** written in the **T** position can be used for words beginning **multi**.

multi-storey   multiplication   multi-racial

NATION/NON
A big loop, representing two **N**s and filling most of the space between the two writing lines can be used for words beginning **nation** or **non**.

nationalise   nation-wide   nonsense   non-smoker

non-payment   multi-national

Exercise 28.1
Read the following sentences:

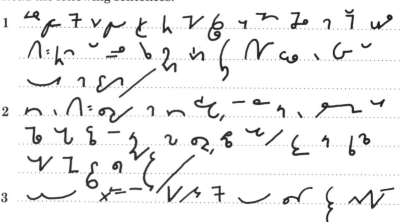

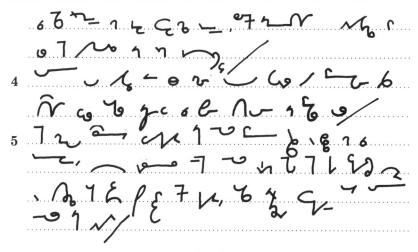

SEMI

Use a Teeline **S**, on the line, disjoined but immediately in front of the rest of the word.

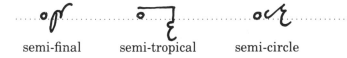

| semi-final | semi-tropical | semi-circle |

SUPER

Use a Teeline **S** with the **U** indicator, disjoined and written above the rest of the outline.

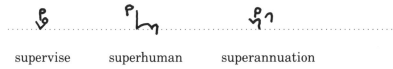

| supervise | superhuman | superannuation |

Exercise 28.2

Read the following sentences:

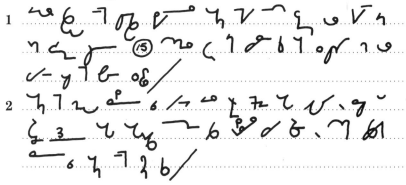

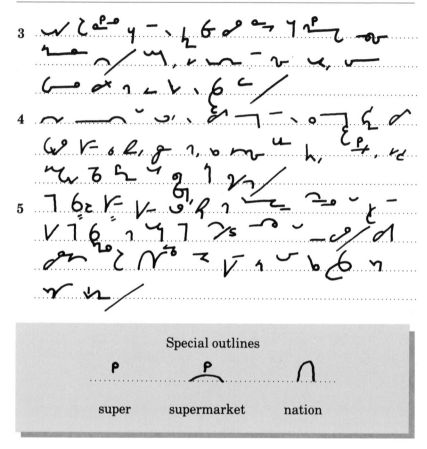

3

4

5

Special outlines

ρ   ρ   ∩

super   supermarket   nation

Exercise 28.3
Read the following sentences:

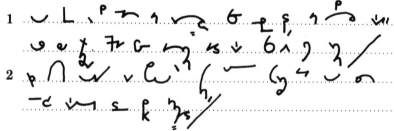

1

2

Dictation practice
Read the following passages and prepare for dictation.

1 Day out for the family

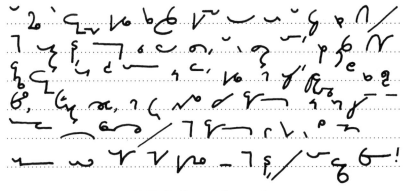

2 Pollution of the earth

3 Company concern at poor English

Full vowels as word endings

Full vowel A

The word **able** is represented by the full vowel **A**: ..⋀..... Until now the words **able/ability** have only been used standing by themselves or in word groupings, but the sign can also be used as a disjoined word ending, written close to the rest of the word to represent **-able** or **-ability**.

capable/capability   reliable/reliability   desirable/desirability

viable/viability   acceptable/acceptability

Other endings can be added:

-S: tables   cables   valuables

-ING: cabling   tabling   labelling

-ED: cabled   labelled   tabled

Full vowel **A** with the **I** indicator added for **Y** ..⋀.... represents **-ably**.

reasonably   honourably   favourably

Word groupings

unable to   enabled to

Exercise 29.1

Read the following sentences:

1

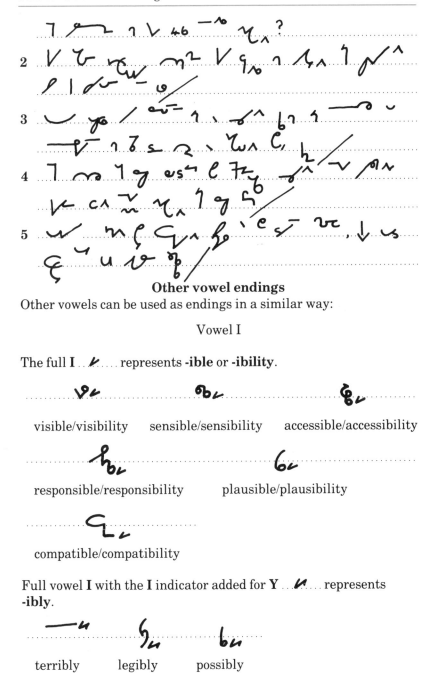

Other vowel endings

Other vowels can be used as endings in a similar way:

Vowel I

The full **I** .. 𝘷 .... represents **-ible** or **-ibility**.

visible/visibility   sensible/sensibility   accessible/accessibility

responsible/responsibility   plausible/plausibility

compatible/compatibility

Full vowel **I** with the **I** indicator added for **Y** ... 𝘷 .... represents **-ibly**.

terribly   legibly   possibly

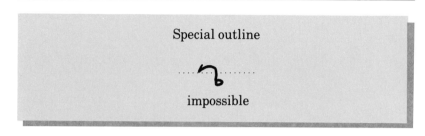

Special outline

impossible

Exercise 29.2

Read the following sentences:

Full vowels O, E and U

Other endings and the **I** indicator for **Y** can be added to all these.

Full vowel **O** ..**O**.. represents **-ob(b)le** or **-ouble** or occasionally **-obility**.

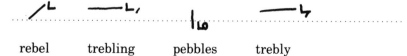

noble/nobility   trouble   troubled   rouble   doubling   doubly

Full vowel **E** ..**L**.... represents **-eb(b)le** or **-ebel**.

rebel   trebling   pebbles   trebly

Full vowel **U** … **u** …. represents **-ub(b)le** or occasionally **-ubility**.

voluble/volubility	soluble/solubility	bubbles	volubly

Exercise 29.3

Read the following sentences:

1

2

3

4

5

Dictation practice

Read the following passages and prepare for dictation.

1 Motoring abroad

2 The Post Office

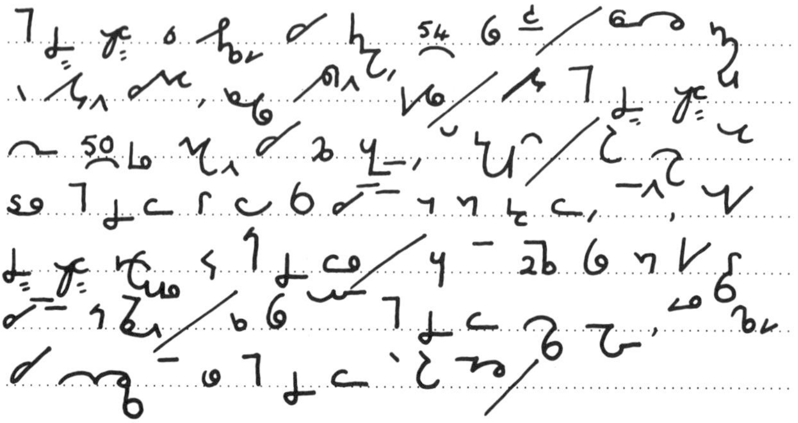

3 Drinks in the office

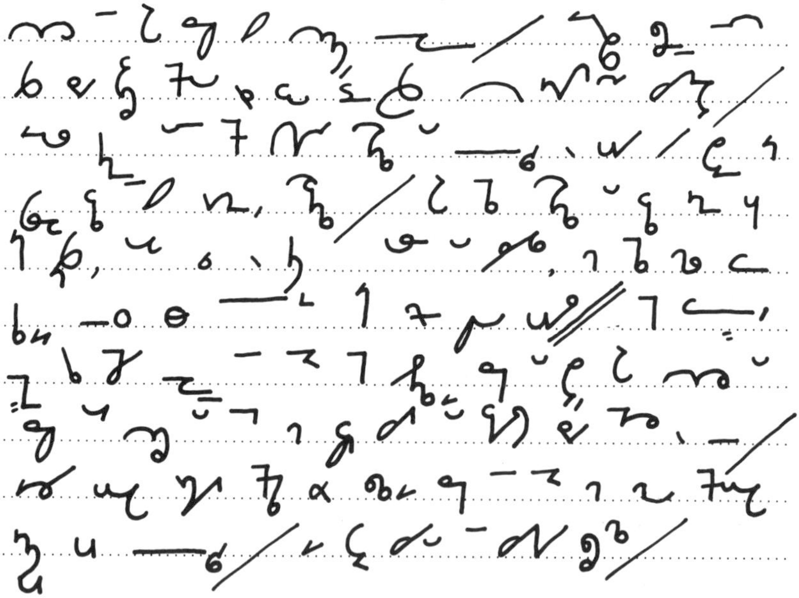

When **R** follows immediately after **B**, **C** or **G**, you can condense the outlines by writing the next stroke through the previous letter and omitting the **R**.

BR

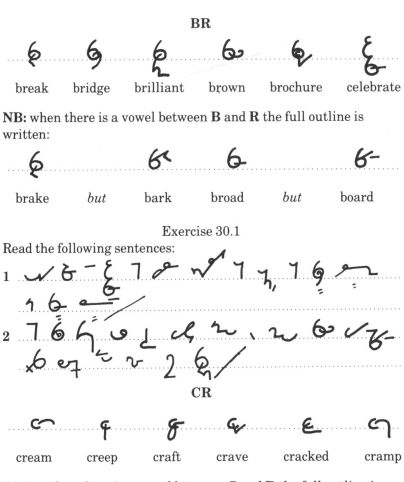

| break | bridge | brilliant | brown | brochure | celebrate |

NB: when there is a vowel between **B** and **R** the full outline is written:

| brake | *but* | bark | broad | *but* | board |

Exercise 30.1

Read the following sentences:

1

2

CR

| cream | creep | craft | crave | cracked | cramp |

Again, when there is a vowel between **C** and **R** the full outline is written:

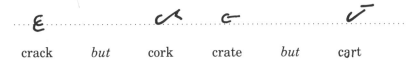

| crack | *but* | cork | crate | *but* | cart |

Exercise 30.2

Read the following sentences:

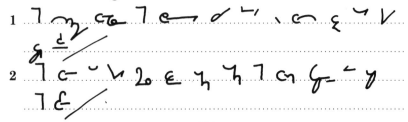

GR

| green | group | grave | grow | ground | undergraduate |

When a vowel occurs between the **G** and **R** the full outline is
written:

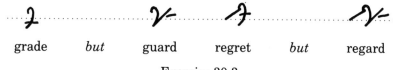

| grade | *but* | guard | regret | *but* | regard |

Exercise 30.3

Read the following sentences:

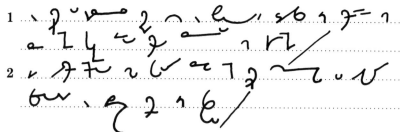

Sometimes you may find it is easier to write words in full

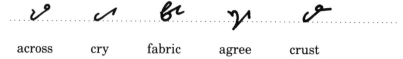

| across | cry | fabric | agree | crust |

For easier reading back, write **T** near to the top of the previous
letter and **D** nearer the bottom:

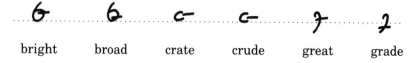

| bright | broad | crate | crude | great | grade |

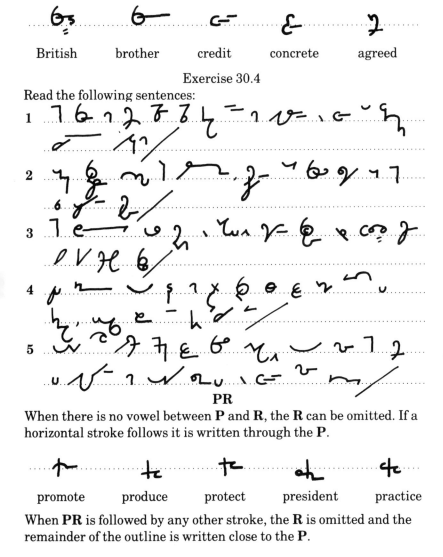

British   brother   credit   concrete   agreed

Exercise 30.4

Read the following sentences:

1

2

3

4

5

PR

When there is no vowel between **P** and **R**, the **R** can be omitted. If a horizontal stroke follows it is written through the **P**.

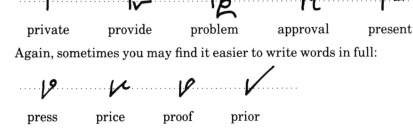

promote   produce   protect   president   practice

When **PR** is followed by any other stroke, the **R** is omitted and the remainder of the outline is written close to the **P**.

private   provide   problem   approval   present

Again, sometimes you may find it easier to write words in full:

press   price   proof   prior

Exception

The **R** principle is not used when words already have disjoined endings:

bring   branch   prince   crucial   expression

Exercise 30.5

Read the following sentences:

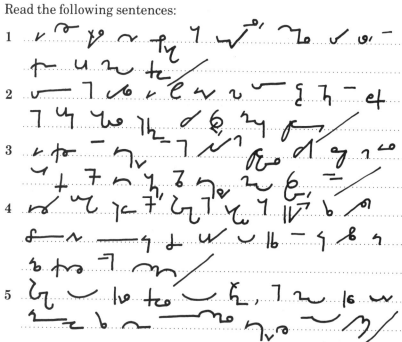

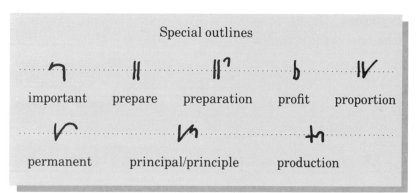

Special outlines

important   prepare   preparation   profit   proportion

permanent   principal/principle   production

Exercise 30.6

Read the following sentences:

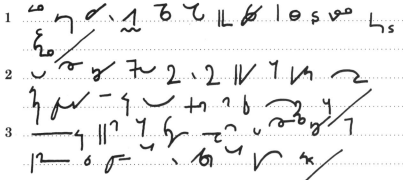

Dictation practice

Read the following passages and prepare for dictation.

1 Memo from Production Manager to Personnel Manager

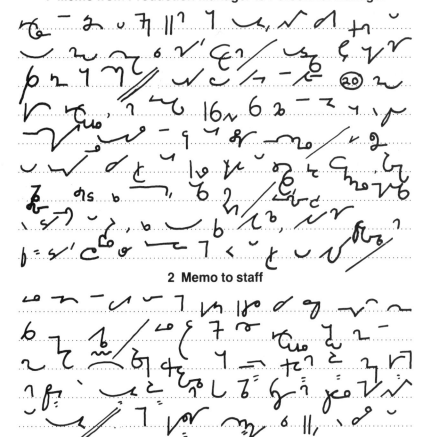

2 Memo to staff

[shorthand notation]

3 Letter from a bank about a new service

[shorthand notation]

Unit 31
The R Principle – AR, OR, UR

When a word begins with the vowels **A**, **O**, or **U**, followed by **R**, you can use the **R** principle. Condense the outline by writing the consonant following the **R** through the full vowel.

AR

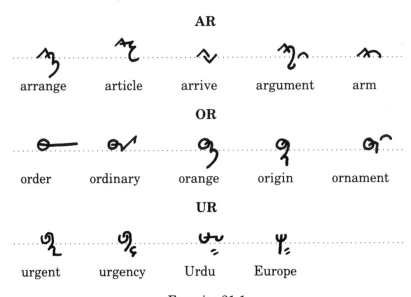

| arrange | article | arrive | argument | arm |

OR

| order | ordinary | orange | origin | ornament |

UR

| urgent | urgency | Urdu | Europe |

Exercise 31.1

Read the following sentences:

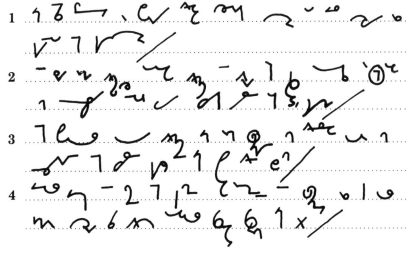

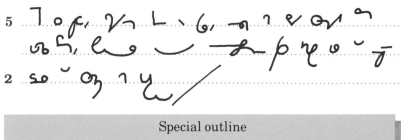

5 ...

2 ...

Special outline

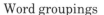

organisation

Word groupings

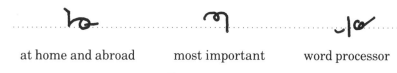

at home and abroad   most important   word processor

Exercise 31.2

Read the following sentences:

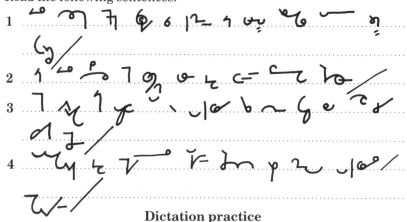

1 ...

2 ...

3 ...

4 ...

Dictation practice

Read the following passages and prepare for dictation.

1 Memo from the computer department

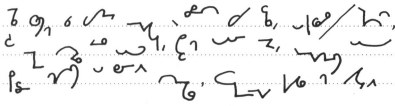

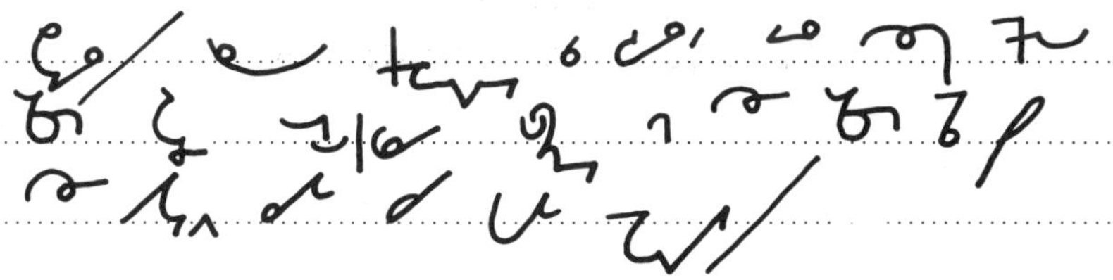

2 Letter about a bring and buy sale

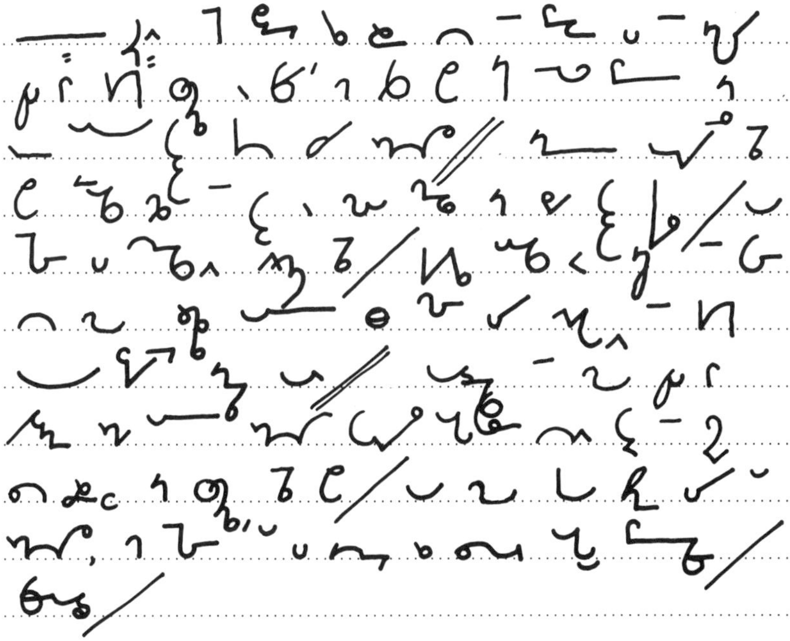

3 Response to questionnaire

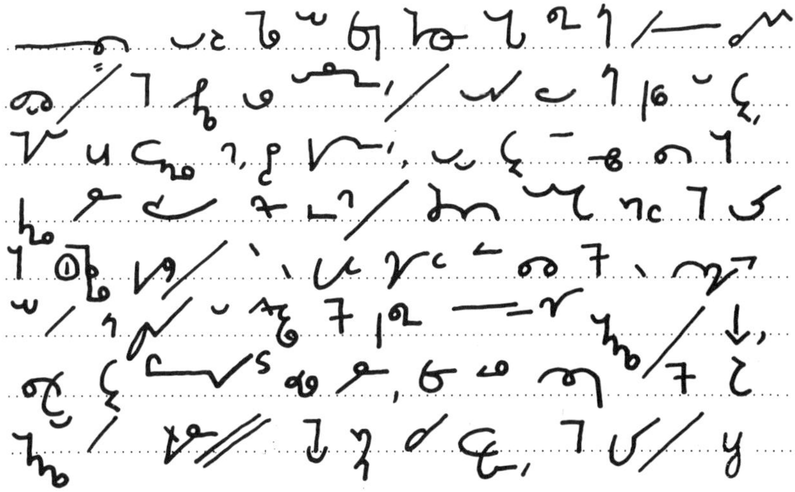

Metric measurements are easy to write in Teeline; just follow these simple rules:

Weight

Gram: when it follows a figure, use a Teeline **G**.

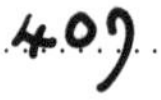

...*4.0.* .... 40 grams   ...*3 .* ..... 300 grams

...*225.* ..... 225 grams

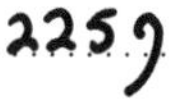

If you need to write the word on its own, use the outline ...*.* .

Kilogram: this can be reduced to **KG** as in

.....*.* ..... 1 kg   ...*.* .... 1/2 kg

Length

Metre: use the **MR** blend written in the **T** position.

...*.* .... 1 metre   ...*.* .... 5 metres

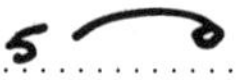

...*.* .... 4 metres

Centimetre: the **CN** and **MR** blends can be used in the **T** position.

...*.* ..... 5 centimetres

Millimetres: **M** and **MR** in the **T** position.

...*.* .... 5 millimetres

Kilometre: use the **K** and **MR** blend.

...*.* .... 5 kilometres

Capacity

Litre: use the **LR** blend written downwards.

...*4.* ... 4 litres   ...*10.* ... 10 litres

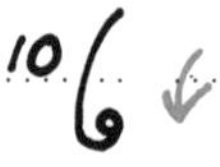

Millilitre: use **M** and the **LR** blend written *upwards*.

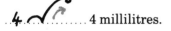   4 millilitres.

Exercise 32.1

Read the following passage and prepare for dictation.

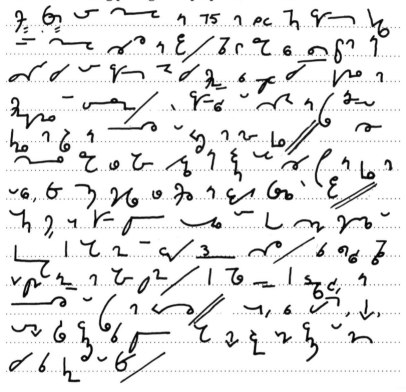

Congratulations on reaching the final unit! You should now be
ready to turn over and try some longer dictation passages.

Finale

Now read the following pieces. Remember, the faster you are able to read the passages, the more quickly you will be able to take them down as dictation. Then practise any outlines or word groupings you are not familiar with before using the passages for dictation. If you are to succeed you will need to practise the difficult outlines first. Why not try the passages at a variety of speeds, perhaps starting at 40 wpm? When you can get a complete note at 40 wpm try the piece again but this time at 50 wpm and so on.

Dictation practice

Read the following passages, practise unfamiliar outlines or groupings and then prepare for dictation.

1 Memo to company car drivers

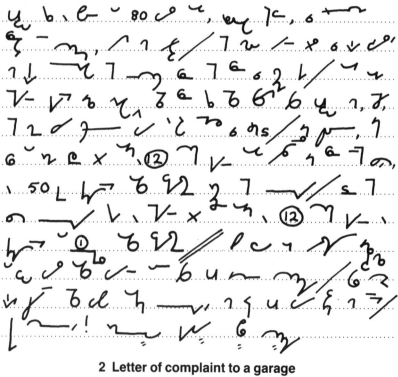

2 Letter of complaint to a garage

[Shorthand text]

3 Notice to departmental managers

[Shorthand text]

4 Letter from headteacher to parents

5 Letter to residents about estate vandalism

If you were able to take down and transcribe the previous passages, why not have a try at this last piece? It is only short, so maybe you will be able to achieve 80 wpm!

Christmas notice in department store canteen

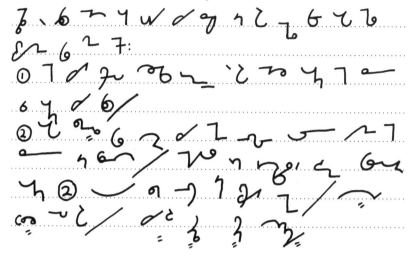

1 INTRODUCING THE TEELINE ALPHABET
Exercise 1.4

so   no   us   ox   up

Exercise 1.5

do/day	he	letter	your	south
we	go	to	be	me
kind	a	and	very	pence/page
electric	are	from	you	eye/I
accident	able/able to		question/equal	

2 WRITING IN TEELINE
Exercise 2.1

Employers expect applicants for secretarial posts to be skilled in all aspects of office work, including shorthand, typing, word processing and office procedures.

Teeline is easy to write and read and fun to learn. You must understand, however, that as well as writing Teeline as quickly as you can, you must transcribe your shorthand speedily and accurately. Always have a dictionary on your desk and remember to use it.

Exercise 2.2

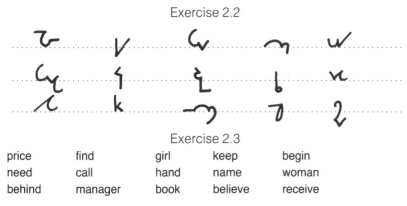

Exercise 2.3

price	find	girl	keep	begin
need	call	hand	name	woman
behind	manager	book	believe	receive

These are only some of the words you may have written down – there are many other possibilities.

Exercise 2.4

1 Do you need to type a letter to him?

2 It is 5 o'clock and time to go home.

3 They had an accident in a car park.

4 If I had an opportunity I would like to go with you.

5 Your manager left to hire a car from a garage.

6 Will you accept an opportunity to join her company?

7 They will go with you to see her.

8 It is a good joke and it made me laugh.

9 Will you deal with your mail from some agents?

10 A woman told me about a good book in a book club sale.

11 I am not able to accept a figure in your account, so you will need to amend it.

12 If you will give me an opportunity, I will tell you how I paid your account.

13 It is 12 o'clock and I am able to get an account book from him.

14 If you are able to type some letters until 5 o'clock I will give you a lift home.

3 ADDITIONAL TEELINE CHARACTERS
Exercise 3.1

1 I wish to purchase the chair I saw last week in your shop.

2 If you go to visit the school they will go as well.

3 We shall require some Dutch cheese if you go to the shops.

4 Do not give them the opportunity to change the electric goods.

5 I shall go with you to cash the cheque.

Exercise 3.2

1 I believe we shall see some bargains when we go to the sale.

2 The blue car was in the garage when the paint was damaged.

3 While we are in the park we shall eat in the big café there.

4 It is an ideal day to go out to visit the old church.

5 The ship from the south was in the harbour.

Exercise 3.3

1 Why was the rep at the office today at 4 o'clock?

2 Who will give the letter back to me?

3 Let us go out while it is daylight.

4 Where was the garage in York where we saw the good cheap car?

5 Will we see your manager when we go to Greece?

Dictation practice

1 Who will call at your shop to check the damaged chairs etc?

2 Will you take your cheque book when you go to purchase some clothes?

3 The paint we shall choose is light blue.

4 The kind girl from the agents will take you to visit the Show House.

5 While I was in the book shop I saw some very good bargains.

6 There was an accident near the Ship Inn today at 2 o'clock.

7 I shall take the parcel of old clothes with me. Where is it?

8 Why not take the old papers from the desk to give you some space.

9 I got a digital watch from the shop near the park.

10 When I get back I will show you the video of Jean and me in Wales.

11 They missed you at teatime when they dashed out to get some fish and chips.

12 Why will the manager of the shop not be able to see you today?

13 The coffee from the machine was cold and had a bad taste.

14 It was some time ago when we last had the opportunity to see you.

4 S AND PLURALS
Exercise 4.1

1 If you leave your car it is wise to keep it in sight.

2 It is said your school days are the best days of your life.

3 I called in the shop near the office and purchased a magazine.

4 The girl will need to take the letters to the main post office if they are to catch the last post.

5 When I get some spare time I shall paint the garage again.

Exercise 4.2

1 When you go to the shops be sure to get me some eggs and, if you are able, perhaps some fish and cakes.

2 I told the boss I shall go to Leeds to see him and I will need to reserve a sleeper if I am to reach his office in time.

3 These cakes are not as good as those I saw last week at the shop in the Square.

4 I was amused to hear of his success in the latest show.

5 We are amazed to hear she has been dismissed from the business as she seemed to be a very good typist.

Dictation practice

1 A day in Paris
Some of the girls at the office will not be / able to take this opportunity to go to Paris with / us. I do wish they could all go. A day / in Paris makes very good sense to me at this / time of year. (**43**)

2 Memo to office managers
To all office managers – From today the staff are not / to take snacks while at

their desks. Will you make / sure all the typists and sales staff are told this /. It looks very bad and has to stop. Is this / a business office? It looks to me like a snack / bar. From today all staff will get time off at / 11 o'clock and 3 o'clock if they wish to go / and get a cup of tea. **(76)**

5 WORD GROUPINGS: 1
Exercise 5.1
1 We will be finished in a minute and we shall leave the office soon.
2 That was a good opportunity to visit the butcher's shop.
3 I am sure you will see the latest models at the garage as soon as possible.
4 Do you mean to do that?
5 Show me the letter as soon as it reaches the office.

Exercise 5.2
1 I am able to visit the old church at teatime today.
2 We will be able to join them as soon as possible.
3 We should be able to close the business deal at 3 o'clock today.
4 Will you be able to discuss these accounts with us?
5 This company believes he is able to do his job well.

Exercise 5.3
1 Have we received those accounts today?
2 We have chosen a male sales person, who should be able to join us in June.
3 They have the latest figures and he is able to check them.
4 We should have received the letter this very day.
6 I have finished the questions I was told to do.

Exercise 5.4
1 The messenger should have been told to deliver the goods as soon as possible.
2 The post should have been here sooner than it was.
3 Perhaps we may be able to see you as soon as we have received the letter.
4 The price of office desks could have been a lot less.
5 He missed the bus and this will be the reason why he is so late.

Exercise 5.5
1 The teacher and the lawyer gave the girl some good advice.
2 With the aid of the shopkeeper, he chose the carpet.
3 The manager of the hotel was very kind to them.
4 The use of post codes is advised by the Post Office.

5 We will be able to take the car to the garage near the mosque as soon as possible.

Dictation practice
1 Opening of hotel
I am sure that this hotel chain will be able / to open its latest hotel at the end of June. / As soon as it is finished, the business person will / be able to book in and receive the very best / service. We are sure it will be a success and / may be of use to you and your company as / well. (**61**)

2 Sales notification
We have just received a letter to the effect that / all the items from his list are still sold at / the old price. We are told that he is able / to pack and ship the goods to us as soon / as the request is received. The postal charges are the / same as last year. (**54**)

3 Paying for books
The last Spanish book has been received and also the / final bill. This account will have to be paid as / soon as possible and I shall be able to send / the cheque to them today. I am so glad I / was able to purchase the books as I use them / with the class all the time. (**56**)

6 WORD GROUPINGS: 2
Exercise 6.1
1 I would have thought it would be correct to send the parcel to me today.
2 The girl searched until she saw a desk made of oakwood to give to her office manager when he left the company.
3 When Edward and I leave the office at the end of the day we are able to finish the crossword puzzle; I do like to be able to put in the last word.
4 Would you be able to go to get the reward at the George Hotel if they give it to you?
5 I am sure they would have gone towards the park to fetch firewood but it would have been an upward hike to get there.

Exercise 6.2
1 I agree that we need to open an office in the north and I am sure you will be able to manage it if you would accept the job.
2 In these days of higher prices we would be well advised to keep charges low and it would be good business to change the figures in the lists we send out.
3 In those days, a man was paid to do a job; a woman was paid less if she had the same job.

4 James was enthusiastic when he was told he would have a good business opportunity in the north of Wales.
5 She must have been very careless to have had an accident of that kind in the office.
6 In these days we have a lot of clothes made from synthetic wool and they look just as good as the genuine cloth.
7 They have been in the school hall all day as they wished to raise funds in aid of the hospice.
8 He was ninth in the class although he thought he should have been higher and in that case he would have had a prize.

Dictation practice

1 Memo to staff
Miss Jones is to leave the company at the end / of the month because she wishes to go to live / in the north again. We would love to give her / a gift when she leaves, and I hope you would / all wish to give towards it. Would all those who / care to, see Miss Smith as soon as possible. (**59**)

2 Office machinery
Some time ago I had a job in an office / that had no electric devices of the kind we have / today. In those days I typed letters with a manual / machine, and I managed to reach a speed of 50 / words a minute. These days, I have lots of electrical / aids in the office to give me a hand and / they make life a lot easier. (**66**)

3 Advertisement
We need a person who has good office skills. Would / a post in the Sales Office of a big business / in the north appeal to you? Are you keen and / enthusiastic? Are you able to type well at 40 words / a minute? Do you wish to be a success and / be paid a good sum at the end of the / month? If you do, then we need to hear from / you as soon as possible. (**75**)

7 T AND D
Exercise 7.1
1 When you send your cheque to me will you be sure to date it.
2 The estate agent sold the detached house last week.
3 He hesitated when we told him the price of the car.
4 The Sunday paper he requested was sold as it was midday and it was too late.

5 We told the teacher we had studied the business passage she gave us to do last night at home.

Exercise 7.2

1 We will wait outside the school at 11 o'clock as we must be in time to catch the bus at midday.
2 At the same time as you send out the letters today will you attach the notice of those dates when we shall be closed.
3 They said we could have a rebate if we settled the account as soon as possible.
4 The man at the garage told Kate that the damage to the car was not too bad and he said that it would take a week to repair.
5 There was an accident at the baseball game today when the ball hit a man and knocked him out.

Exercise 7.3

1 Within the last week we have had a message from John to tell us that he will meet us some day soon.
2 We need you to be with us when we visit the boutique as we will need your immediate advice when we make the purchases.
3 Monday is a bad day to go to the shops with you as I have to be at the office that day.
4 Without the lift in your car we would not have managed to get to the office in time.
5 What is your name and what details have you requested?

Dictation practice

1 Memo to hotel manager

I would like to make an immediate visit to the / hotel to see the kitchens. As soon as I have / seen them, we will be able to discuss the details / and make a choice of microwaves. (**36**)

2 Note about missed meeting

The sales manager, Kate Smith, will not be able to / go with us as she is in the north that / day. As you state, this is a missed opportunity, but / I will send her details of the account as soon / as possible. I am sure that you will be able / to meet her some day soon. (**56**)

3 Changes in car park

Within the last hour I have received a letter from / the office manager. She would like to meet us all / in her office at 4 o'clock today to discuss what / changes need to be made in the staff car park. / I believe she wishes all staff cars to be parked / in the spaces allotted to them. (**56**)

8 Y AT THE END OF A WORD;
Y IN THE MIDDLE OF A WORD
Exercise 8.1

1 Ray and Jenny say they will go to watch the relay race with me.
2 It will be very busy at the rugby match so I will stay at home where it is quiet.
3 In his letter he says 'do not delay, buy today.'
4 I believe that we are out of stock of the sherry you wished to buy but we should have some in again soon.
5 I shall be happy when it is pay day as I need some money to buy a pair of shoes.

Exercise 8.2

1 The boy has to hand in the essay to the teacher by Monday at the latest.
2 I am sure Roy said it just to annoy me.
3 The boys enjoyed the game and asked if they could stay to see the rest of the show.
4 When the shop manager asked what had happened the girl was very loyal and said little about the cycle accident.
5 The little boy gasped with joy when he was told he could have as many toys as he wished.

Exercise 8.3

1 I am sorry to say that I shall be late at the office but I will stay behind to make up the time should it be necessary.
2 When you have seen my estimate will you pass it to Roy immediately as he is in a hurry to copy it.
3 It is beyond me why the electricity bill is so high this month.

Dictation practice

1 Problem of unpaid bill
I am sorry to say that the electricity will be / cut off if we do not get the bill paid / by Monday. It is quite beyond me why you could / not pay the account when you called at the office / last week! (**42**)

2 Note from headteacher to his assistant
In case I should not be at school at any / time, perhaps it would be best if you keep my / keys in your desk. If this should happen at a / time when you are busy, I am sure the senior / boys will assist you should it be necessary. (**48**)

3 Overtime request
Roy – as always, I shall be very busy at the / end of the week and will have to stay behind / at the office if the accounts are to be posted / in good time. I am

sorry to ask, but will / you be able to stay late and give me a / hand when the rest of the staff have gone home? / I will take you home in my car immediately we / are through although it should not be very late. **(79)**

9 MORE ABOUT VOWELS
Exercise 9.1
1 We will be able to visit my old aunt at tea-time today.
2 He will have the opportunity to audit the accounts some time this month.
3 The average age of the class last August was 12 years.
4 There was an accident in the area about 2 o'clock so the coach was very late.
5 She wished to get away immediately and did not stay to the end of the show.

Exercise 9.2
1 Details about the car sales have been released in the latest business magazine.
2 Have you noticed that the office has been equipped with all the latest automatic models?
3 The last episode of the TV serial will be repeated yet again at the end of the year.
4 The Senior Buyer always attempted to equate the aims of the business with the end results.
5 The Royal Opera Company will visit opera houses in the north, as well as the south, this autumn.

Exercise 9.3
1 The electricity bill is due to be paid at the end of the month.
2 I usually manage to finish the questions by 3 o'clock.
3 I shall easily deliver the August issue of the magazine within the necessary time.
4 We will be able to use the car to take the electric machine up to the Royal Hotel.
5 I was upset to hear that they will not allow us the usual rebate.

Exercise 9.4
1 This memo should be sent not only to the Head of Accounts, but also to the Office Manager.
2 You ought to pass on my message and my cheque to one of the cashiers.
3 Anyone who wishes to set up a business in a shop or office will not usually have an easy task.
4 The only paper that told us about the rail crash in Rome was the *Daily Post*.

5 It appears that the individual share issue was immediately a huge success.

Dictation practice

1 Installation of lifts

The lifts in the office block ought to be installed / in the early days of May. I am sorry about / the delay and I shall have to ask you all / to accept my apologies. We usually take three weeks, so / we are due to finish at the end of the / month. These lifts will need an individual service check-up / only one day a month. **(65)**

2 Staff Club Account

It is only about a year ago this autumn that / it was decided to set up this staff club. You / all await my account and I am delighted to be / able to give you the figures on the year's business / as we meet today. We have easily pursued the aims / we established and we have managed to do a lot / in the past year. I am happy that you all / made use of the club and gave us your loyalty /. **(80)**

3 Choosing a car

We have so many models of cars in the showrooms / these days that it is not very easy to decide / what make of car one should purchase. The average U /K car is kept about 2 or 3 years only / and then it is usual to have a change of / model. The latest issue of the Car Magazine will not / only assist anyone about to buy a car, but will / make it easy to make the best individual choice. **(79)**

10 VOWEL INDICATORS AS WORD ENDINGS
Exercise 10.1

1 If you will take the opportunity of checking the books, I will willingly send you to the South East office in a month's time.

2 I hope you will soon be visiting the manager of the shop and showing him the model we have made.

3 There will be two meetings going on in the Sales office on Tuesday and I hope you are all willing to go to them.

4 I am saying that you should not leave awkward queries until the end of the day or you will be late going home.

5 If you hear the enquiry bell ringing when you are typing, it is necessary to answer it immediately, and not keep anyone waiting.

Exercise 10.2

1 I am sorry but I am no longer able to send you the items you requested as I am having to change my methods in respect of selling electric goods to your business.

2 The manager wrongly accused the young boy of stealing the goods and selling them to some girls along the way to school.

3 I am having to type a lengthy estimate and it is taking me longer than I
   thought it would.
4 That coat belongs to me and ought to be on the hanger where I usually leave
   it.
5 At the annual show it was lovely to hear the singer who sang some happy
   songs, and also to listen to the hand bell ringers clanging their bells with
   enthusiasm.

Exercise 10.3

1 I am sending you many things made in Kenya and nothing should be
   damaged because all things in the parcel are well wrapped and are made of
   metal.
2 I wish to say something to the staff about the way goods are handled when
   they are sent outside the area.
3 There are some very good things on sale in the shop and staff will be able to
   buy anything they wish at 8 o'clock.

Dictation practice

1 Notice of meeting

There will be a meeting of all staff in the / Buying office on Thursday at 10
o'clock. We have many / things to discuss and I shall be sending you an /
agenda when it has been typed. If there is anything / anyone would wish to add,
see Miss Young who will / be happy to amend it. (**55**)

2 Memo

Memo from Sales Manager to Sales Persons
I have just   received the latest individual sales figures. It / seems that takings
have risen quite a lot this year /. It is going to be a demanding task to keep / this
up. I am asking you to put all your / energy into visiting and phoning buyers.
The personal touch is / really necessary. I hope good things will develop from
all / your enquiries. (**62**)

3 Memo

Memo from Manager to Staff
It has been decided to / make the car park bigger by using the space belonging
/ to the company at the back of the building. Not / only are we changing the
hedge to railings, but a / single barrier will be erected where cars go in and /
out. At the Leisure Park the path behind the swimming / pool will be lengthened
and a longer jogging course will / be added. Nothing will happen until the end of
April / and I am sorry that the car park will then / be closed until the job has
been finished. (**98**)

11 VOWEL INDICATORS TO EXTEND WORD ENDINGS
Exercise 11.1

1 The wrinkled bank manager spent most of his time thinking about what had caused his boat to sink in the English Channel last week.
2 When you think about it, you realise that it costs nothing to thank someone when they have been kind to you, and then perhaps they will assist you again.
3 Could you tell the manager that the lady who purchased the chunky pink jumper says it has shrunk in the wash, and she is demanding her money back.
4 We sell goods to the zoo and when I deliver there I usually spend a while watching the monkeys, donkeys, minks and skunks.
5 If the business is to rank amongst the best in the UK, we must not have any weak links in the senior staff.

Exercise 11.2

1 We will ensure that we send out goods to agents immediately and also check that all the items are enclosed in the parcel.
2 I am happy to have the opportunity of doing business with your company in Hong Kong and perhaps you would be so kind as to enclose your latest list of individual stock items when you answer my letter.
3 Thank you for your cheque which was enclosed with the letter you sent dated 4 May telling me about the accident your sales person had in the north.
4 Thank you for your letter, received on 9 June. I shall be happy to accept the post of junior in your accounts office.
5 At the meeting the chairperson gave a vote of thanks to those who had decided to raise money to give to the old folks home.
6 Thank you for your enquiry dated 12 May and the enclosed cheque.
7 When we send goods to purchasers we enclose the packing note inside the parcel as we think it is safer than when it is stuck on the outside.
8 I think I must say a very big 'thank you' to the rest of the staff who have always made me think that I was one of the team.
9 Thank you for your cheque received in the post today, and as requested the goods will be despatched to you immediately.

Dictation practice

1 Letter to a potential customer

Thank you for your enquiry dated 25 July. We / sell high quality ladies' and girls' clothing of all types / at very low prices to selling outlets, mainly in the / north.

We enclose a copy of the latest booklet and / price list, and would suggest you note the many bargains / on page 3. We hope to hear from you soon /. (**60**)

2 Letter about a meeting

Thank you for your letter about the meeting on Monday / when we shall be discussing my repairing and painting business. / You have requested a map to find the way from / the edge of the estate to my office, but I / think it will be necessary to fetch you in my / car. We really ought to take the opportunity to stop / at the Royal Hotel on the way back to have / something to eat. Perhaps you would give me a ring / in a day or two and let me know what / you think. (**92**)

3 Extract from a talk on office duties

No two jobs are the same, so when you join / a business you should find out what the job entails /. Among the duties you may have are opening the mail /, answering the phone, typing, receiving enquiries, and keeping details of / meetings. You may also be requested to do some book- / keeping, and to receive and pay out cash. If this / is the case, it will be necessary to keep the / money secure. It may also be one of your tasks / to take the money to the bank. You must always / do your best, listen to your boss, and accept the / good advice of the rest of the staff. (**108**)

12 WORD ENDINGS -NCE, CH AND -NCH
Exercise 12.1

1 It is quite a distance from my home to the office building.
2 It is a nuisance but I need a silencer on my car as I am not able to use it as it is.
3 We have a vacancy in the book shop to suit a young person and all things being equal we might get one who likes books.
4 It is a long distance to Wales from your house in the north but I hope some day we will be able to go there.
5 We must take a chance on booking the hire car in June and hope we will have saved the money by then.

Exercise 12.2

1 Since the correspondence sent by the agency did not get here until midday today, it must be sent back to them immediately.
2 Have you noticed the change in the admittance charge at the dance hall? I believe details such as this should have been announced at the last dance.
3 We asked to see the manager of the agency because each of us has had very little assistance from the staff.
4 While you are at school you will find many books in the library which will assist you as you are behind with your science studies.

5 I think we should go out to lunch today as the staff luncheon club is charging too much at the bar.

Exercise 12.3

1 The insurance on the car my son has bought will be too much to pay so in the circumstances I will pay the difference.

2 Once I had told the girl the circumstances would be different from her last meeting with us she realised at once she must change her attitude.

3 The shop sells such things as clothes, china and toys and each day there is a sale of goods in aid of the hospital.

Dictation practice

1 Rebate on electricity account

A rebate is due to us if we pay the / electricity account immediately. This is different from the usual bill / which makes it necessary to take it to the office / as soon as possible if we wish to have the / rebate. Will you take it at once, since we missed / the date once last year. **(55)**

2 Hotel booking in Paris

I enclose details of the leisure weekend vacancies and cost / of insurance requested by you in your letter which was / received in this office today. You have asked to be / booked into a small hotel in Paris where lunch is / served each day. Hotels of this kind are not easy / to find in Paris as it is usual to eat / in cafés where such tasty meals are served. **(68)**

3 Sales meeting

I have lunch with the Sales Manager each week. It / is such a nuisance having to put up with such / things but in the circumstances I am not able to / avoid it. I do not enjoy the lunch very much / but at least it makes no difference to my diet / as I do not eat too much when I am / there. **(61)**

13 FORMS OF F AND L; F BLENDS

Exercise 13.1

1 When it was very cold last year we had lots of fun skating.

2 It was a fine, sunny day when we climbed the hill, but I admit that we had some help from the police team who are very good on the high slopes.

3 I am sure you are enjoying your Teeline and I would like to think you are fitting in at least one lesson a day.

4 I am fed up with the postman who calls at my house because he is always so late with the mail.

5 My face is looking spotty today and as three of my colleagues at the office have measles, I think that perhaps I am getting it too. I do hope not!

Exercise 13.2

1 Am I on the right road to get to the business park at Westgate?

2 The old cart rattled along making a deafening noise.
3 I am very happy to hear that this school will be teaching my child reading and writing at an early date.
4 My favourite food is fish and chips and I often have them when I have been to the squash club.
5 I nailed the estate agent's card to the notice board and in doing so hit my finger at the same time.

Exercise 13.3

1 I shall be flying to France for a short holiday in February when I hope to get some fine, sunny days and lots of good food.
2 Small boys used to enjoy flying kites but it is not often you see them doing so these days.
3 To get to the holiday resort by car and ferry takes half a day so we have decided to fly instead despite the cost of the fare.
4 The girls really enjoyed helping the family with the hay making.
5 The fibres in this fabric are faulty and I refuse to pay for it.

Exercise 13.4

1 Referring to the letter I sent you last week, will you book me a first class ticket on the 10 o'clock flight to Paris on Friday.
2 With reference to your letter about fitting a telephone in your company car, I am sorry to say it will be Friday at the earliest before I have the opportunity to do so.
3 All sorts of things seem to have gone wrong since I joined this firm and I have had no success at all.
4 There are lots of business letters to write and forms to fill in these days when you have a farm.
5 With reference to your holiday request, it is not the first time I have had to remind you that it is not satisfactory for three typists to be away from the firm at the same time and, therefore, I am refusing your request.

Dictation practice
1 Refuse collection from flats

For a long time those of us who live in / the flats at the end of Park Road have felt / that we are being ignored by the men who are / supposed to collect the refuse. We should have the rubbish / collected each week but we are lucky if the dustbins / are emptied once a month. At holiday times we have / to use cardboard boxes because the bins are full. We / are not getting a satisfactory service. Last week we saw / rats in the passages and, I may say, this is / not the first time this has happened. (**97**)

2 Why are business letters so boring?

Sometimes I think that business letters are very boring. Do / they really need to be this way? I realise that / they have to have a date and a reference but / does the language need to be so formal? For instance, / why do they always have to begin with the phrase / 'With reference to your letter' or 'Thank you for your / letter'? I am sure I could think of all sorts / of things to write in a first class letter. It / would be amusing and easier to read if I had / my way. Good chiefs should think about this before they / dictate their letters. (**103**)

3 Problems of shared telephones

It is not satisfactory that four girls should have to / share one telephone. There have been some cases of 'flu / in the office and this has not been helped by / staff having to share telephones. Germs are able to spread / fast enough without giving them a helping hand. Each of / us should have a telephone and I am going to / tell the manager what I think about this. I suppose / he will say that the firm is short of money /. We have all heard that tale before and will not / fall for it again for we have just typed the / forms showing the figures for the first half year accounts /! (**110**)

14 WORD ENDINGS -MENT AND -SELF
Exercise 14.1

1 Payment for the one-page advertisement in the local paper is due today, but the amount will be quite small.
2 At the last moment the individual government departments issued a revised statement on the latest development in the affair.
3 A Member of Parliament may use the photocopier in the basement of the Houses of Parliament at any time.
4 The last time we visited the agency was when we had to find staff to join the management team.
5 All his requirements are in fact being met, therefore he is in favour of going ahead with the agreement immediately.

Exercise 14.2

1 His judgement is first-rate and he has built up his business from nothing into a huge empire.
2 As it is so hard to get staff the manager himself helps in the bar at lunchtime.
3 The sales person herself suggested we wait for the latest model, which should be in the showrooms by the end of January.
4 I myself would like the chance to join the opening ceremony, but I realise that you need me here in the office.
5 They helped themselves to some car stickers, which appeared to be free.

Dictation practice
1 Flight bookings

The advertisement should state that we have reserved seats to / many cities on some days of the week on scheduled / flights. Most of the saving made by the company is / passed on to the clients themselves. At the moment we / also offer flights on different airlines on different days of / the week and prices for these are quoted on request /. Clients should get in touch with us as soon as / possible and let us have their requirements immediately before circumstances / change. **(81)**

2 Daydreaming

I saw an advertisement in the local press about a / job in a government department. At the last minute I / decided to write off enclosing the necessary details about myself /, thinking perhaps in due course there might be an opening / helping my local Member of Parliament in his office. In / a few weeks I fell back to earth with a / bump as I had a letter to say the post / had been filled. As I enjoy my typing job and / get on well with the management and staff I do / not really mind and feel glad I am staying where / I am happy. **(103)**

3 Report on holiday village

The holiday village was built only last autumn, but bookings / for this development for the month of August are good. / Last-minute spring bookings are also satisfactory. The individual apartments / are well equipped to meet all the clients' requirements and / the activity area is a real asset. There is a / well-stocked shop selling many things which is open from / 8 am to 8 pm each day and / the snack bar will in fact be open for 2 /4 hours. We are all very happy with developments so / far and hope that your agency will do its best / to help us in the busy season. **(107)**

15 WORD ENDINGS -SHUN, -SHL, -SHIP
Exercise 15.1

1 May I make the suggestion that we vote on this motion before we have the election of the officers?
2 Following the resignation of the fashion designer, the corporation will need to appoint a sufficiently skilled person from an agency.
3 We must take immediate action if we are to fight off the opposition whose operations are taking a bigger portion of sales in televisions.
4 We have made this revolutionary machine to the highest specification and I have no reservations about selling it.
5 The efficiency of the section is being questioned, and one of the things we must do is to change the system of requisitioning stationery.

Exercise 15.2

1 I myself believe that it is essential to have a satisfactory relationship with all the staff in the department.

2 Each month the firm holds functions in the social club and we watch the special acts.

3 When you fill in the form do not write your initials but put your name in full in block capitals.

4 The official mentioned that although the firm is to close, it is crucial to avoid hardship amongst the staff.

5 We are especially happy with the decision we made to purchase the additional equipment for the Research and Development Department.

Exercise 15.3

1 The electrician has just told me that the electrical equipment in the office, and in particular the photocopier, needs immediate attention, and therefore we must get it looked at as soon as possible.

2 I would like you to give your attention to the financial state of the company because it seems we are having difficulty with one of the specialist items we manufacture.

3 It is my intention to change the way we operate the specialised manufacturing side of the business with immediate effect.

Dictation practice

1 Memo from machine shop manager to foreman

I would like to bring to your attention the fact / that the specialised presses we have acquired will be set / up the week before the Spring Bank Holiday. The electrician / has suggested that he could do the electrical part in / the holiday, but he requires someone to help him. We / must pay particular attention to health and safety as required / by law. (**62**)

2 Letter to bank manager

At the moment I am having difficulty manufacturing sufficient goods / to meet the demand of buyers. I am in a / position where I need additional specialist machinery. It is my / intention to purchase different pieces of equipment and to do / so I need financial assistance through a bank loan. I / am enclosing the loan form and I would be glad / if you could give this your immediate attention. (**68**)

3 Memo from sales manager to sales staff

I have just received notification that the cost of the / goods we sell has risen by a third. The situation / is that we are not able to absorb these costs / and we have no choice but to put up prices. / I think we have sufficient stock left to carry on / with the special offers until the end of the month, / but following that we must put into effect the prices / on the attached list. The catalogue and price list will / be amended accordingly. (**83**)

16 T AND D BLENDS
Exercise 16.1

1 We will travel straight to the terminal after lunch to make sure we are in time to meet your flight from Madrid.

2 The lesson on social history was easily the most interesting we have heard this term.

3 I will drive to your daughter's address as early in the day as I am able to as I do not enjoy driving in the dark.

4 It would be much better if we do not make the trip to Scotland during the school holidays when the roads are so busy.

5 A telephone call disturbed the electrician as he was making a difficult repair to the lights in the dress shop.

Exercise 16.2

1 These days holiday-makers tend to buy tiny gifts to give after returning home as they are so much lighter to carry.

2 The entertainment at the dinner dance held by the Social Department was first class and therefore it was a pity there was such a very poor attendance.

3 During the visit to London we shall attend a museum and visit a theatre and if there is time we will then have dinner at a restaurant.

4 The pattern of development in the Modern History Department is satisfactory. In particular, there is a trend towards specialist qualifications.

5 While the roads are being widened in some parts of Doncaster there is some difficulty in dealing with the drainage.

Exercise 16.3

1 We thank you for your order which we received yesterday.

2 In order that we may send the photos to your relations could you let us have their names and addresses.

3 In order to make sure that your name and address appears correctly on the notepaper you require will you check this copy.

Dictation practice
1 Queen's Birthday Parade

Last time we visited London we managed to obtain seats / to watch the Queen's Birthday Parade. This was very special / and the entertainment was unique. There is an amazing sense / of history about the occasion as well as the tremendous / sight of the regiments of troops keeping in time with / the military bands. In the circumstances it must be something / of an endurance test for the soldiers and the horses /. (**70**)

2 Traders' Association

Thank you for your letter received yesterday and for returning / the form with the names and addresses of the traders / in your street who are determined to deal with the / nuisance of litter outside their shops. A meeting will be / held to discuss this matter as soon as we have / all the names of those interested. We are hoping to / attract the attention of all the traders in this part / of the city before the end of February and this / should then give us some influence particularly in dealing with / the local refuse firms. **(94)**

3 Memo to tour operator
Would you be able to send the attached form to / the clients who spoke to us on the telephone yesterday / in order to find out their travel requirements? Also enclose / a leaflet for information on tours during the month of / August. These will be for first class travel only and / should appeal to those who are interested in the good / things in life. The specialist hotels we are using this / year are all of the very best quality and most / have sports facilities and indoor swimming pools. In order that / we may book as soon as possible perhaps you could / give this matter your immediate attention. **(106)**

17 BUSINESS GROUPINGS
Exercise 17.1
Letter about damaged goods

Dear Sir

Thank you for your letter about the damaged / items you received in your order last week. We have / seen the stereo you returned, and agree that the fault / was caused through poor packing. We apologise for this and / in the circumstances we are enclosing a refund cheque with / this letter, as requested.
Yours faithfully. **(56)**

Exercise 17.2
Letter about a job application

Dear Madam

With reference to your letter dated 15 June, / I write to inform you that we have no vacancies / at the moment. If you would like to fill in / the enclosed form and return it to me, I will / put your name on the waiting list and will let / you know if a vacancy occurs.
Yours faithfully **(58)**

Exercise 17.3
1 We must always remember that the reason for being in business is to make money, and this means that generally all members of staff must do their best to achieve this necessary aim.

2 It should be a general rule that the minimum stock levels are checked on a daily basis.

3 I generally telephone the members of the Board before a meeting so that they will remember the time it begins.

Dictation practice
1 Letter about an Annual General Meeting

Dear Member

The Annual General Meeting of the Sports Club / will be held on Friday, 24 January at 8 / o'clock. As a member of the Club, you are requested / to attend and vote for the officers to be elected /. I enclose the agenda, and hope to see you then /.

Yours sincerely (**52**)

2 Letter about charging for carriage

Dear Sir

Thank you for your order, which is being / despatched today. As you will realise, up to this time / we have generally made no charge for carriage. In order / to reduce costs, we must charge a minimum amount in / future for any sale. The scale of charges is enclosed / with the revised price list.

Yours faithfully (**57**)

3 Letter about a holiday enquiry

Dear Sir

I enclose the information for the train holiday / about which you enquired yesterday. This 4-day trip starts / in London and takes you to the north of Scotland / with various short stops along the way for sightseeing. Passengers / may enjoy the beautiful scenery of the landscape without a / care. It is indeed a superb holiday and one you / will always remember.

If I may be of further assistance, / do not hesitate to telephone me.

Yours faithfully (**78**)

4 Letter about an electrical shop

Dear Sir or Madam

I am happy to announce the / opening of my electrical retail business in your district. I / have all sorts of general electrical goods in stock, and / I am sure you will not find better prices in / the area.

I enclose with this letter a voucher which / will allow you to purchase any item for less than / the normal retail price.

Remember the store is open from / 9 am until 6 pm from Monday to / Saturday. Hurry along yourselves to see my selection today.

Yours / truly (**91**)

18 THR BLEND, CTR, RN; G or J AND -NESS
Exercise 18.1

1 I rather like the singing of the pop star we heard last night.

2 Each day I am going through all the Teeline theory as fast as I am able to although finding the time is rather difficult.

3 The weather will be quite cold in the Alps so I must remember to take some sweaters and long thermal tights.

4 There is going to be a film show at the village hall tonight so perhaps I will see you there.

5 The spectators gathered on the terraces long before the match was due to start.

<h2 align="center">Exercise 18.2</h2>

1 The modern trend is to cater for youngsters who generally seem to have a lot of money to spend.

2 The handbag I liked most of all was made of red leather with a long strap – I rather hope my mother will buy it for my birthday.

3 One fact we must keep in mind is that this is not the first time these young boys have been in court.

4 I am earning enough money from my part-time Saturday job to pay for a holiday where the sun shines and it will not rain.

5 These days it is usual for both mothers and fathers to share in the bringing up of their children and I think this is quite correct.

<h2 align="center">Exercise 18.3</h2>

1 One of the forwards was carried off with a major injury just before half-time.

2 The girl at the bank seems to be all 'sweetness and light' but she does not fool me for a single moment.

3 It saddens me when I think how beautiful the garden was before the storm spoiled all the trees and shrubs.

4 I do believe that neatness is a virtue and I do try to be neat but my family say I am very untidy.

<h2 align="center">Exercise 18.4</h2>

1 During their honeymoon in southern France my son and his wife found that their spending money was going further as they did not eat lunch in first-class restaurants.

2 As you are not able to be there on Saturday perhaps we shall be able to get together some other time.

3 I like fish and chips but, on the other hand, I do not enjoy the smell of them when somebody else is eating them.

4 We seem to be travelling farther away from the path and I think we should go no further.

<h2 align="center">Dictation practice</h2>

<h3 align="center">1 Waiting for hospital appointments</h3>

There is nothing quite so annoying as having to wait / in a queue for a hospital appointment to see a / specialist. Surely there must be some other way of doing / things. To sit for hours watching patients pass by and / with only an old magazine or newspaper to read, is / no joke when you have either to rush home to / meet the children from school or return to the office. (**70**)

2 Down Memory Lane

A few weeks ago I met some old friends I / had not seen for a long time. They told me / that their home had been in the southern part of / Spain for the last ten years but during their absence / they had always had affectionate thoughts of their old village /. I took the opportunity to show them round the old / estate where we all used to live as boys but / sadly the only buildings they recall are the parish church / and the railway station. (**84**)

3 Letter cancelling a meeting

Dear Harry

Further to my telephone call of yesterday, I / am sorry that I shall not be able to attend / the meeting in London on Thursday. I have three other / appointments on that day which I am not able to / alter. If you will telephone my office during the week / we may be able to agree on another date. I / do hope so.

On the other hand, to avoid the / long train journey into London perhaps we could meet at / a half-way point. I have to be in Leeds / on Friday and shall be there all day so perhaps / we could get together for a drink and lunch at / the Red Dragon? Yours (**114**)

19 BLENDS: LR, MR, WR, WK AND WRK
Exercise 19.1

1 There is a very popular clearance sale of colourful clothes for children at the local department store.

2 As she was still a learner she was told her salary would be smaller than that of other machinists in the factory.

3 We need fuller details of the general development on the large site near the library to be able to give a fair and clear report.

4 Is there a large scale car park near the docks where lorry drivers are able to park to wait for their Channel ferry?

5 Your enlarged colour leaflet is very popular with the members but we need to be able to give them fuller details of the cost of many items.

Exercise 19.2

1 Customers need more details of what is on offer on the Capital City two-day summer holidays.

2 We have a customer interested in the market garden we have for sale but he will require a large mortgage.

3 We thought the merger of the food merchants would solve all their difficulties but the directors did not get on together.

4 As it was such a marvellous morning we decided to walk much further to the marina by the sea.

5 It is clear that the marriage is not to be, it is just a rumour.

Exercise 19.3

1 I worked very hard in the garden to make the flower beds attractive for summer.

2 We walked along the lower floor of the warehouse where the electrician was working by himself.

3 The queue to enter the Houses of Parliament was worse than usual last weekend.

4 As a young child my memories of summer are that it was always sunny and warm with clear blue skies.

5 It will be interesting to learn how the workman is getting along with the machine the manufacturer installed in the factory.

Exercise 19.4

1 Dear Ms Webb, As we were not able to meet this morning could we meet in my office tomorrow? You must bring with you the sum of money required as a deposit. Yours sincerely

2 Dear Miss King, Our business of sending flowers is getting larger and larger and we send our flowers by post to all parts of the world. Let us send yours. The first bunch will be free. Yours sincerely

3 When we bought the cars we thought it was more or less worthwhile but we are changing our minds and believe more and more that the sums of money paid were more than was necessary.

4 The world appears to be smaller and smaller as we ourselves are able to travel to parts of the world which were once difficult to visit.

Dictation practice

1 Letter about a repair to a tap

Dear Sir

I would like to draw your attention to / the dripping stop tap in the street outside this house. /

As there has been very little rainfall in our part / of the world during the whole of the past year / it is annoying to say the least that this water / is being allowed to run to waste.

Will you therefore / give this matter your immediate attention and I hope to / see the workmen from your department before very long.
Yours / faithfully (**81**)

2 Answering the telephone

Today there are more and more occasions when the telephone / seems a nuisance. Despite all the benefits it brings such / as being able to speak to friends and relations in / all parts of the world, help in emergencies, and lifelines / for the elderly it does have some drawbacks. It takes / a strong will to ignore a ringing phone. It could / be crucial. Perhaps there has been an accident or someone / is injured or in difficulties. We always stop what we / are doing in order to answer the phone. We leap / out of baths or leave the chip pan on or / perhaps cut short the world's worst row, and it is / then usually a wrong number. Maybe it would be worthwhile / buying an answer phone so that we could lie in / the bath for a larger and larger part of the / day and make believe we are out. (**147**)

3 Opening a florist's shop

Dear Mrs Walker
With reference to your letter which I / received this morning, we have some shops for sale but / our stocks of empty units are getting smaller. I enclose / details of the ones we have. As you would like / to open a florist's shop, I suggest you ought to / visit the shop in the latest development in the High / Street which I think may be more or less what / you require, as there is a very large frontage where / you would be able to set out your flowers. I / hope you will like its individual position; this particular shop / is two doors further along from the bank.
Perhaps we / could meet tomorrow morning at 11 o'clock to visit the / shop together and talk about the minimum sum of money / that you may require as a deposit. I look forward / to our having a successful meeting.
Yours sincerely (**148**)

20 NUMBERS, CURRENCIES AND COLLOQUIALISMS
Exercise 20.1

1 You may book any one of the 200 outside or 100 inside cabins on board the liner.
2 This year we anticipate that 1000 travel agents will be joining us for the annual reception on board.
3 Only last week scientists found pottery believed to be 100 000 years old.
4 The sun is some 5000 million years old, and the earth is 300 to 500 million years younger.

5 The population of London has risen to almost 10 million.

Exercise 20.2
1 You would be well advised to buy the painting at the auction tomorrow; the minimum asking price is less than £1000.
2 The first child, 12 years and below at the date of travel, receives a 50 per cent reduction when sharing a room with 2 adults.
3 The big Wall Street crash in 1929 affected most parts of the world for many years.
4 Our local estate agent is offering a house for sale on the other side of the Channel for 200 000 francs.
5 The airline suffered a net financial loss of almost $22 million during the last 4 months.

Exercise 20.3
1 A large number of offices have been moved from the capital city in order to reduce rents.
2 I'm not surprised that Blackpool is the number one tourist attraction outside London.
3 We're eager to change our French francs back into sterling, as we're not going there again for another year.
4 He's visited all parts of the world as a representative of his government.
5 I would like to draw your attention to the fact that a number of business letters took 4 days to reach their destination.

Dictation practice

1 The holiday market
This half of the 20th century has seen the development / of mass tourism to all parts of the world. This / season they have had a rise in holiday bookings of / 15 to 20 per cent. As the pound is strong / against the French franc and the dollar, tour operators generally / have been able to offer special deals such as 2 / weeks for the price of one in France and the / USA. On the other hand, holiday prices for / Germany have remained steady. (**84**)

2 Tourism in France
Nearly 45 million foreign travellers visited France last year, / 5 million in July alone and 4 million in August /. Earnings from the holiday trade will reach £50 million / before the end of this record year which saw 30 /000 more jobs in tourism. The number of air passengers / from the UK rose to 1.5 million, / up 12 per cent, and cross-Channel figures are also / up with a 24 per cent rise. The French / Government Tourist Office will therefore be spending £2 million / on its

advertising in the UK in future years. / Magazine, trade press, TV and poster
advertising will have / to be looked at again. (**115**)

3 French skiing holidays

Dear Madam

Thank you for your interest in our advertisement / for French skiing holidays.
It's not surprising that skiers love / France, since it offers such a wide choice of
runs / and resorts. The number of visitors to the slopes has / gone up by 10 per
cent and is set to / rise further. So whether you're a beginner trying to stand / on
your skis or you've already mastered the sport, France / is the skier's number
one destination.

A French skiing holiday / doesn't mean just skiing. For a change it's easy to /
have a look round the shops, go to the skating / rink, try some hang gliding or
go to a café / where hot chocolate and coffee are served at all hours / of the
day.

Our latest information pack is enclosed and / we look forward to hearing from
you again soon.

Yours / faithfully (**141**)

21 X BLENDS
Exercise 21.1

1 My sister was so badly cut when she dropped the Pyrex dish that she had to
   go to hospital for an x-ray to see if any of the glass was still in her leg.
2 I think you should try to exert some influence on him as soon as possible
   otherwise he is likely to be expelled from college.
3 The manager of the Bell and Bottle hotel is trying to get a drinks extension so
   that the party will not have to finish early.
4 My parents are hoping to book a luxury cruise to the Far East and Australia
   to mark the occasion of their retirement from business.
5 Because I was ill at Christmas my husband and children had to cook the
   Christmas dinner without me – it was an experiment they are not likely to
   attempt again.

Exercise 21.2

1 A number of firms operate flexi-time for their workers these days and this is a
   big help for young mothers with children at school.
2 We hired a firm of experts to build the extension and they have done an
   excellent, if expensive, job.
3 The electric mixers at the exhibition seem to be very useful but do you think I
   shall be able to achieve the same excellent results as the demonstrator?
4 A fax machine in an office is not an expensive, executive toy, but a vital piece
   of modern equipment.

5 When the shop assistant examined my electric iron he found it to be in an extremely dangerous state because the flex was badly frayed.

Exercise 21.3

1 If you are going to get maximum marks in your nursing finals you will need lots of experience on the hospital wards, for example, before sitting the examination.

2 I expect that you have been told again and again how dangerous it is if you exceed the maximum speed limit when driving on the motorways.

3 Except for the odd occasion when it has slipped my mind, I have stuck to the exact amounts in my diet and my waist line is looking quite trim.

4 It is extraordinary that my sister will be taking the French examination at the same time as I expect to be sitting my German examination.

5 In my experience, examination passes do not always indicate high flyers. For example, the office manager has very few qualifications but he is excellent at his job.

Dictation practice

1 A visit to the dentist

No-one enjoys paying a visit to the dentist. It / is an experience all of us could well do without. / The initial examination is bad enough but I think it / is the fact that we are not sure exactly what / to expect that makes us anxious. We may think there / is nothing wrong with our teeth but the dentist has / an extraordinary way of finding that all sorts of things / need attention. On the other hand, if we have extreme / pain we are glad to have the offending tooth extracted. (**90**)

2 Foreign currency exchange rate

How is it that when I go on my holidays / the exchange rate for currency is not in my favour? / Last year visitors going to France got the maximum number / of francs to the pound for 10 years, but because / I am going this year the rate has dropped and / is approximately 1 franc less. That extra franc would have / made a big difference to the amount of money I / had to spend. The next time I decide on a / trip to foreign parts I shall have to do some / forward thinking and get my currency well in advance if / necessary when the rate is in my favour except that / I do not always have the money so far ahead. / (**120**)

3 Noticeboard announcement of sponsored walk

There is to be a sponsored walk on Saturday, May / 3 in aid of St John's Hospice and I expect / all the staff to make an effort to take part. / It should be an easy way of not only raising / much-needed funds for the hospice but an opportunity for / us to get some exercise. Of course I realise that / some of the accounts department for example, will be exhausted / before they reach the half-way stage but they will / be suffering for a good local cause!

The exact starting / time has yet to be announced, along with the target / distance, but I am assured this will not exceed 20 / miles. I suggest we start training next Friday in the / lunch hour. I will be at the main gates at / 12 o'clock and I am expecting you all to be / there!

No exceptions will be made or extraordinary excuses accepted. / Remember, positive thinking is the key to the enterprise.

Richard / Bird

General Manager (**163**)

22 CM BLENDS
Exercise 22.1

1 The computer link used by the holiday company is an asset especially when booking hotel accommodation.
2 The committee recommends the immediate start of the advertising campaign.
3 It is not uncommon to find in the first year of trading that expenses far outstrip income.
4 We welcome the scheme to accommodate unaccompanied minors in a special departure lounge.
5 It is essential not to comment at this stage, as this particular difficulty might affect the outcome of the meeting.

Exercise 22.2

1 I expect the forthcoming Social Committee meeting to discuss our recommendations.
2 This export company was established by ourselves in competition with 4 other similar commercial firms.
3 I have come to the conclusion that communication skills are some of the best assets in commerce.
4 He became an income tax specialist and a member of the Finance Committee.
5 We are looking for a combination of skill and experience in commerce in our computing staff.

Dictation practice

1 The English seaside

Fifty or 60 years ago millions of day-trippers a / year came to the English seaside, but the number of / visitors dropped in later years, although the seaside is today / making a comeback. The travel business is making sure that / those who go to the coast are generally offered excellent / facilities. Some holiday resorts once had dirty beaches, but there / have been many campaigns to clean up all the beaches /, as well as the waters along the coastline and as / a result things are changing for the better. Some beaches / in the UK have received tidy beach recommendations and / others have received the highest award for clean beaches, the / Blue Flag award. **(113)**

2 Tourism survey

A survey amongst 50 leading holiday companies shows just how / necessary it has become to offer better visitor care in / future years. It reported that it was essential to make /'sure that visitors come back to the UK. Terminal / 4 at Heathrow Airport was praised as being very clean / and the staff very friendly. The companies said that tourism / is facing stiff competition from other parts of the world /, where accommodation is often more satisfactory and gives up-to- / date comforts. Typical comments were for example: 'The quality of / the welcome at our airports and in tourist resorts must / get better. Staff should be more welcoming and remember that / a smile costs nothing.' **(114)**

3 Classification of accommodation

Dear Mrs Southern

Thank you for your enquiry. You are / correct in saying that when you are away from home / on business, it is necessary to choose the kind of / accommodation that suits your requirements and to which you look / forward. Until the home Tourist Boards started classification schemes, / choosing accommodation was always difficult and you had to rely / on what friends told you.

Today, there are 3 schemes / covering accommodation. The first scheme covers hotels, motels, guesthouses, etc / and it guarantees certain standards of service. Each establishment has / been checked and classified at one of 6 levels. The / next scheme covers self-catering in cottages, bungalows, flats etc / while the third scheme deals with holiday chalets and camping / parks. With these schemes there ought to be no difficulty / for anyone to find exactly the kind of accommodation needed. /

Yours sincerely **(152)**

23 N AND V BLENDS, NW AND WN, WORDS BEGINNING EV
Exercise 23.1

1 In a letter to the solicitor the vendors stated that the kitchen units were solid oak, but in fact they were only oak veneer.

2 When the inventory was checked it was discovered that goods to the value of £1000 were missing.

3 The venue for our meeting tomorrow about the trip to Venice has had to be changed because vandals have damaged the community hall.

4 I am a novice when it comes to making out invoices, but Vera has been teaching me exactly how to do them.

5 If you wish to become involved in voluntary work come to our charity shop; we are looking for someone with your commercial skills.

Exercise 23.2

1 It is a wonderful feeling owning our own house, and we are having a bottle of wine to mark the occasion.
2 For safety reasons it is unwise to store volatile liquids near a source of heat. They should be in sealed bottles to ensure they do not evaporate.
3 Every year everyone in the business is invited to attend a dinner and dance, and the event is always a success.
4 We would like all your unwanted items to sell at our winter jumble sale; we usually find that everything is sold quite quickly.
5 Yesterday, the vintage car was left on the verge with its windows down to allow for ventilation as it smelled very musty.

Exercise 23.3

1 There is no doubt at all, in our opinion, that the majority of our clients will remain with us when we go to the lovely new office building.
2 We know several reasons why a number of staff in your company leave when they have been there for only a short while and in our view you should be more friendly towards them.
3 You have fastened page 4 of the report upside down and as the meeting is at 2 o'clock I would like you to change it for me now.
4 There are several lively girls coming today from the local college to get information about the new job we have advertised at headquarters.

Dictation practice

1 Letter of complaint

Dear Sirs

Our 3 new delivery vans were delivered from / your works today. When the vehicles were checked, however, it / was discovered that the sign of our manufacturing company logo / has been put on one of the vehicles upside down. / In our view, if the van is used as it / is, our competitors would very quickly use this error to / their advantage.

We are behind with our deliveries as it / is, so we are sending the van back today for / immediate correction.

Yours faithfully (**84**)

2 Letter about a carnival

Dear Mr Bell

As you know, I am on the / town's Carnival Committee, and I am writing to local firms / to ask them if they would like to take part / in next year's event. I am sure

that in your / company you have several men and women who would be /
happy to come along in fancy dress or maybe take / part in the show. This year
we had some lovely / costumes and some lively novelty acts, and I expect next /
year's event to be even better.
Yours sincerely (**88**)

3 Notice to staff

Several members of staff in the department have expressed a / desire to start a
first aid class. In our opinion / everyone should have this opportunity and we
have now found / an experienced teacher who is willing to give lessons to / a
maximum number of 15 persons.
No doubt you will / all want to take advantage of this chance to learn / a new
and valued skill. If you do, add your / name to the list on the staff noticeboard.
However if / more than the specified number wish to be involved, there / will be
another course later in the year. (**98**)

24 C AND N BLENDS, INS
Exercise 24.1

1 It is a scandal that such an extensive convention hall has been built in the
valley as it has quite spoiled the lovely view.
2 Perhaps we should have a quiet conversation together about the new
scheme for the conference when I visit your company next week.
3 I believe the consumption of chocolate bars in the canteen has been
expanding in the last few weeks.
4 I remember the large canvas marquee that was hired for your wedding
looked beautiful when it was full of flowers.
5 In our experience we generally find London to be the most central situation
for meetings of reps from all parts of the country.

Exercise 24.2

1 It was inconsiderate of the cinema manager not to encourage his staff to
take extra instruction in their work.
2 The consequence of the economic situation in New Zealand is the smaller
and smaller amounts of interest we are now earning on our investments.
3 In our view it would be an uneconomic gesture on your part to insure with
another company when you have had an insurance policy with us for so long
and have such a large no claims bonus.
4 We hope such controversial discussions with a member of your staff will be
kept to a minimum in future.

5 The editor was totally unconcerned by the scandalous nature of the reports in the local newspaper.

Exercise 24.3

1 I can remember how convenient the train journey was when we travelled recently to Paris, can you?

2 There is a sale today at the country manor house in the village and they are giving a discount which will be discontinued tomorrow on some items.

3 We travelled by taxi across London for convenience but we can't do this often as the fare is very expensive.

4 We can let you have several tickets for the flower show but if the date is inconvenient we can't guarantee to change them.

5 Until this century, efficient methods of communication were unusual. For instance, we cannot imagine life without telephones; they are now part of everyday life.

Dictation practice

1 Jury Service

Some of you may one day be asked to serve / on a jury. This is a vital job and you / are obliged to attend for Jury Service unless you have / some special circumstance for not doing so; for instance, if / you have earlier convictions or jail sentences or if you / are more than 70 years of age. These are some / of the instances when you can be excused and there / are several others when you cannot. The fact that it / may be just inconvenient is no excuse at all. **(89)**

2 Letter to a contractor

Dear Mr Singh

I am writing with reference to the / letter which you sent to me recently about the work / you are doing on my house. Although I know you / are giving maximum time and attention to the job, I / do feel you must now discontinue the work for the / time being as it will not be convenient while I / have an invalid in the house. Later on I hope / you can begin again with the painting of the outside / of the house.

Can you let me know if I / am entitled to a discount on the work not finished /, as you mentioned recently.

Yours sincerely **(106)**

3 Charity shops

I cannot let you leave our country without taking you / to several of our charity shops. I am confident you / will be able to find some interesting items for sale. / There are certain to be garments that are of good / quality and extremely cheap especially suits for men and clothes / for children. It is also quite likely that we shall / find books and items of china and glass which will / make useful but inexpensive gifts. I can confirm that all / the money taken in the shops goes as a contribution / to the charity concerned. As most of the staff in / the shops are volunteers, it is a very efficient way / of raising money as well as giving a useful service / to the community. (**123**)

25 P BLENDS
Exercise 25.1

1 The report concluded that some South American countries were experiencing such poverty that it had become a world-wide concern.
2 Other people have already completed the attached form to apply for supplementary discounts.
3 Some people think that this is neither the time nor place to discuss such a complicated matter as trade discount, but we shall place it on the agenda for the next meeting.
4 The Director himself supplied several people with the news of the company's financial difficulties.
5 An application for employment with this insurance company should be sent in duplicate.

Exercise 25.2

1 You will be pleased to know that there will be ample scope for us to explore the many applications of the electrical appliances we are introducing tomorrow.
2 It is my pleasure to assure you that this company would be pleased to supply free samples to members of the public on completion of this simple questionnaire.
3 I am pleased to recommend this publication to other people, as it excels in the area of management.
4 We are pleased to know that the boy has been expelled at last without any difficulty or publicity.
5 The issues are rather complicated, so I expect there to be a lot of questions in your reply to this letter.

Dictation practice

1 Reply to customer request

Dear Mr Shah
I have pleasure in supplying you with / the requested operating manual for your new appliance. This latest / manual, which I enclose, has only just been sent to / us by the publisher and I am pleased to be / able to forward it to you immediately. I must applaud / your choice of dishwasher as the one you have

chosen / is a splendid top of the range model and very / popular with the general public. The control panel may look / complicated, but the machine is in fact very simple and / convenient to operate.
I am sure the appliance will give / you complete satisfaction.
Yours sincerely (**105**)

2 Opening hours in public houses

It was with much publicity in August 1988 / that public houses in England and Wales opened their doors / to members of the public for longer hours. It is / pleasing to note that this helps tourism in many parts / of the country. It is not quite the same complete / freedom enjoyed by some places on the continent, but offers / a more pleasant service than the old system. Landlords in / the more rural areas for instance have not applied for / longer hours as there has been little extra trade. Generally, / however, the move has been applauded as a success not / only in terms of employment, but especially in supplying better / facilities for people travelling. (**114**)

3 New public toilet

Following many complaints by members of the public, the city / council has just splashed out £200 000 on / its new public toilet. The plush new public convenience next / to the information centre has officially opened its doors. Councillor / Temple said: 'I am pleased to cut the toilet paper / before such a large audience. It was because of the / rise in the number of coach travellers recently that we / realised the need for more toilets in the city and / planning started. We are pleased to know that we now / have one of the most attractive public conveniences in the / southern counties. We shall be pleased to hear of other / people following in our footsteps – we are expecting a chain / reaction!' (**121**)

26 WORD BEGINNINGS – UNDER AND ELECTRO
Exercise 26.1

1 Our catalogue of electronic typewriters which you requested is being sent to you under separate cover.
2 The new electronic equipment is being delivered tomorrow, so could you ask the electrician to make sure the electricity supply is sufficient for our needs.
3 Thank you for your order for an electronic scanner, and we confirm that it has been sent to you today under separate cover.
4 A new underpass is to be constructed underneath the shopping centre and out to the car park.
5 Switch off any faulty machinery immediately, or you run the risk of being electrocuted.

6 Your order for underwear came today and is being sent tomorrow under separate cover, together with our up-to-date catalogue and discount terms.

7 The underscore mechanism on the electronic typewriter needs adjustment, so please ring the technician and ask him to do it as soon as he can.

8 We, the undersigned, wish the management to know that we feel the department is understaffed, and we would like an assurance that something will be done to relieve the situation as soon as possible.

Dictation practice

1 Letter to a hotel about conference facilities

Dear Sir

I am enquiring about the facilities at your / hotel. Our company intends to hold a week-end conference / for approximately 120 people on 17 and / 18 August and your hotel is ideally positioned for people / who will be travelling from different parts of the country / to attend. It is anticipated that most of the people / will require accommodation for one night only.

Could you please / send me details of your rates and any other services / you offer, together with sample menus. I would also like / information about entertainment in the area if you are able / to supply this as well.

Yours faithfully **(107)**

2 Extract from Chairperson's Report

I am very happy to be here today to report / to you the news that we have yet again had / an excellent year's trading. No doubt you are well aware / that our electronic office equipment is the best seller in / the UK, and worldwide sales are on the increase. / I am sure you will be pleased to hear that / dividends are even higher this year than last year.

However, / we must not underestimate the strength of our competitors, who / are undertaking a major advertising campaign at this moment in / time. We must continually invest in new research and development / if we are to keep our position in the market. / **(110)**

3 Letter about laying carpet

Dear Mrs Andrews

Thank you for accepting my quotation for / supplying and fitting carpet and underlay to your lounge, hall / and stairs on 24 March. As you will be / out at work, I understand that I will have to / collect the key from your neighbour, Mrs King. I should / be there around 9 o'clock and the work will be / completed by about 2 o'clock.

I would like to remind / you that you must remember to switch off your electric / underfloor heating on the day the work is to be / done.

If you require any further information, please do not / hesitate to telephone me or leave a message at the / shop.
Yours sincerely (**113**)

27 WORD BEGINNINGS – TRANS AND OVER
Exercise 27.1
1 Larger and larger transporters are coming into this country from overseas and in our opinion action should be taken to limit the speed of these vehicles and not allow them to overtake other traffic.
2 Our manufacturing overheads are increasing each month and we cannot overlook this any longer.
3 The transfer of funds from the bank to the Social Committee is now long overdue and this money is needed for another transaction immediately.
4 We understand you require a translation of some technical papers and if you would let us know the language we will do our best to find an experienced translator.
5 The instructor said it was safe to overtake the large container vehicle in front of us.

Exercise 27.2
1 All over the country and nearly all over the world people are beginning to realise how vital it is to look after the environment.
2 In our opinion we can all do our bit in a small way by reminding children over and over again not to leave litter all over the district.
3 When we went over the Channel recently we travelled by plane and the journey over there was over and done with in less than half the time of going by ferry.
4 We must go over and over the Teeline special outlines to help us to remember them more easily.
5 We spoke to the staff in the Personnel Department but it was necessary to go over their heads and speak to the management.

Dictation practice
1 Overdrawn account
Dear Mr Fiddler
With reference to your account with this / bank we have to inform you that this is still / overdrawn to the extent of £500. Since May / when you transferred your account to us we have written / to you over and over again to notify you of / this financial detail.
In order that we can regard this / matter as over and done with we should be pleased / if you could reduce this overdraft at your earliest convenience. /
Yours truly (**82**)

2 Appointment as courier

Dear Mrs Friend

With reference to your interview yesterday, we / are pleased to confirm your appointment as a courier with / this company. As we mentioned during our discussion, it will / be necessary for you to travel all over the country. / In view of this we supply a company car for / your use. We must point out however, that this is / not for personal use. Therefore, you will be required to / collect the car and return it to the staff garage / after completing each trip.

Yours sincerely **(86)**

3 Extract from Company Report

We are expecting that this year will be another highly / successful one. Our outlets all over the world now number / over 20 serving their own local areas. We have highly / trained specialists. In all these places, they continually advise our / clients on all kinds of company business, for example, valuation / matters. By working in this way, clients receive quick answers / to their questions. We have made good results when developing / the system for overseas financial transactions. Because of this, we / are confident that we shall be able to overtake the / results we attained last year as we shall continue to / offer excellent service and build up a good relationship with / our customers both in this country and overseas. **(118)**

28 WORD BEGINNINGS – MULTI, NATION /NON, SEMI AND SUPER
Exercise 28.1

1 It is a fact that very few people pay their bills on time these days and over the years non-payment of debts has given even large national companies a lot of worry and concern.

2 I am a non-smoker and am unwilling to sit in a restaurant with those who choose to ignore no smoking signs which are placed in positions where they can be seen clearly.

3 We were excited to hear recently that our small local airport is to be extended and electronic communications added, so that international air lines can use the runways in an emergency.

4 Whether we realise it or not our lives are controlled by multi-national companies whose influence is felt nation-wide in countless ways.

5 The new multi-storey car park in the town centre has been a success and is attracting more visitors to the town even though the high charges make a nonsense of the claim from the council that parking will be inexpensive compared with other towns in the area.

Exercise 28.2

1 It was a blow to the football supporters when their team captain was hurt in an incident after 15 minutes play in the first half of the semi-final and was carried off the field semi-conscious.

2 When the new super-store is ready it is expected that it will require a staff of at least 300 who will have been trained by supervisors for about a month before the store is open to the general public.

3 We are all superstitious up to a point but serious study of the super-natural does not interest me. On the other hand, I admit to not walking under ladders for example and I do have a black cat.

4 My dream of winning a free trip to a semi-tropical island for a luxurious holiday is fading fast and, as I am not yet paying super-tax, I think I will have to be content with sunbathing in the garden.

5 The Bank Holiday parade was fun and attracted multitudes of people to hear the bands and watch the multi-racial teams of dancers. For the first time all nationalities took part in what has become an annual event.

Exercise 28.3

1 We had a super time in America but despite shopping in supermarkets everything was so expensive that I cannot imagine I shall ever be able to go again.

2 As a nation we are very slow at learning other languages – we seem to think everyone should speak English.

Dictation practice

1 Day out for the family

In recent years the supermarket with its free parking for / cars and its wide range of goods at competitive prices / has become part of our way of life as a / nation. The weekly shopping trip is now something of a / family outing as the big national chains compete with each / other in cutting prices and offering facilities such as snack / bars, lively music, and play areas for children in an / effort to attract more customers. The children can have a / super time on their own while their parents do the / shopping. What could be better! **(95)**

2 Pollution of the earth

All over the world more and more people are becoming / aware that the huge multi-national chemical companies are the / ones who are polluting our rivers, beaches, land, and even / the air round us. Nations can no longer ignore the / fact that vast amounts of money have been made at / the expense of the environment and that something will have / to be done about it. We exist in a world / where everyone is affected and a super-human effort is / needed if we are to make the world fit for / future generations to live in. **(95)**

3 Company concern at poor English
Memo from Managing Director to staff.

I have come to / the conclusion that there are some members of our company / who are not able to compose a letter without making / mistakes in spelling and punctuation. As a nation we used / to have a fine reputation for our high standard of / education. Sadly, this is no longer the case.

Has no /-one ever heard of commas or even semi-colons? I / should not need to remind you that we are part / of a multi-national corporation and it makes a nonsense / of our nation-wide reputation when correspondence, which is full of mistakes, is going out from the firm.

From today / no letter will leave these offices unless it has been / checked by the departmental supervisor. Therefore, I have purchased dictionaries / for every member of staff. Please use them. **(138)**

29 FULL VOWELS AS WORD ENDINGS
Exercise 29.1
1 Would it be viable to obtain a bank loan, which would enable us to extend the restaurant and have 46 tables available?
2 Her old employer mentioned her capabilities and reliabilty in the favourable reference he forwarded to us.
3 Our offices are situated in a desirable position in terms of transport and this should make a valuable selling point.
4 The members of the staff social committee feel that it would be desirable to have reasonably priced cable television available in the staff canteen.
5 We are unable to supply comparable figures at such short notice, however we shall comply with your request as soon as possible.

Exercise 29.2
1 It is impossible to place this item on the main agenda, but at the same time it would be sensible to discuss the matter under any other business.
2 The open door policy implies that the Head of Department is accessible to all staff at all times.
3 Invisible earnings have risen in the last year which, in our view, allows us to be more flexible about investment.
4 The fax message was hardly legible, but the operator could not be held responsible, as the telephone line itself had been terribly bad.

5 The compatibility of the software with our make of computer is questionable.

Exercise 29.3

1 We were able to double our earnings in the last year and no doubt will treble our earnings in the current year.

2 It is no trouble these days to send a telex, as you can send it directly from your desktop computer to places all over the world.

3 A voluble discussion took place, but we have come to the conclusion that it is impossible to reach a decision without further information.

4 Several members of staff are rebelling about the inconvenient car park restrictions and I am sure these ought to be lifted.

5 I value your noble gesture, but fear that it will not solve this company's financial difficulties.

Dictation practice

1 Motoring abroad

When you drive on the continent, it is sensible to / alter your headlights. You can buy headlight converters at any / reliable motoring shop. In some countries, such as France, it / is also desirable to have yellow tinted headlights. Yellow headlamp / lacquer for painting on your headlights can again be purchased / at most supermarkets or motoring shops. However, you may find / that visibility is slightly reduced, although this is not terribly / serious. **(71)**

2 The Post Office

The Post Office is responsible for handling 54 million / letters each day. Customers enjoy a reliable service, as well / as reasonable prices. Recently the Post Office made £50 / million available for necessary updating of equipment. All mail which / shows the post code can now be sorted on an / electronic coding table, where Post Office employees key in the / post codes. Up to 2000 letters an hour can be / sorted in this way. As letters without the post code / may be delayed, it is sensible for members of the / public to use the post code at all times. **(99)**

3 Drinks in the office

Memo to All Staff from Managing Director

It has been / suggested to me by several colleagues that we as a / company should become more environmentally friendly. It was pointed out / that nationally millions of drinks a year are supplied in / plastic cups from vending machines. All these millions of cups / end up in the bin, which is a huge waste / of resources, and these numbers could possibly double or treble / in the next few years.

The Catering Department has therefore / decided to take the responsible step of supplying all members / of staff with mugs of tea and coffee free of / charge several times a day. I am sure you will / agree that this is a sensible step to take and / know that you will enjoy your drinks. I look forward / to further suggestions. **(133)**

30 THE R PRINCIPLE – BR, CR, GR, PR
Exercise 30.1

1 We are about to celebrate the first anniversary of the opening of the Bridge Restaurant in Broad Street.
2 The brass lamp was packed carefully into a new brown cardboard box so that it would not get broken.

Exercise 30.2

1 The manager criticised the secretary for eating a cream cake with her coffee each day.
2 The crate of heavy goods cracked open when the crane lifted it off the concrete.

Exercise 30.3

1 A group of visitors gave me a flowering shrub in gratitude and said they hoped it would grow strong and healthy.
2 I regret that we no longer stock the green material you require but we have a similar grade in blue.

Exercise 30.4

1 The bride and groom telephoned this hotel today and requested a crate of champagne for their reception.
2 On the breakfast menu at the restaurant, grapefruit with brown sugar on top is offered grilled.
3 The secretary was given a valuable gold bracelet as a Christmas gift from her grateful boss.
4 If you enter our shop and accidentally break or crack any item you handle, you will be asked to pay for it.
5 We very much regret that the cricket bats available were not the grade you required and we are sending you a credit note immediately.

Exercise 30.5

1 I must express my disapproval of the advertising methods you are using to promote your new product.
2 Under the circumstances I feel I have no other choice than to prosecute the youth who was apprehended for breaking into the factory.

3 I promised to improve the recreation facilities for the staff and it is with pride that I am opening this impressive new building today.

4 I am sure you will appreciate that although the value of the property has risen considerably during the past year we propose to keep rises in insurance premiums to the minimum.

5 Although our previous products were excellent, the new process we have introduced has made tremendous improvements to our range.

Exercise 30.6

1 It is important for a representative to be well prepared before he or she visits potential clients.

2 We must ensure that we get a good proportion of the principal market in the north if we are to keep our production and profit margins up.

3 During the preparation of the legal document you must ensure the printer is fitted with a ribbon with permanent ink.

Dictation practice

1 Memo from Production Manager to Personnel Manager

I am pleased to inform you that the preparation of / the working area for the production of our new model / is nearing completion. We should be fully operational by the / end of the month.

We are now ready to recruit / 20 new permanent employees, and it will probably be necessary / to take on a few temporary workers to cope with / seasonal demands. I suggest we advertise for people with previous / experience of assembling electronic components, although this is not essential / as training will be given. I do not think there / will be a shortage of applicants, as our public relations, / recreational facilities and profit-sharing scheme usually attract the kind / of people we require. (**114**)

2 Memo to staff

It is time to carry out the principal proposals for / staff development made by departmental representatives. It is clear that / most employees of the company need to know more about / the practicalities of the Data Protection Act and the Health / and Safety at Work Act and how this legislation affects / their area of work.

The Personnel Manager is preparing a / series of four short sessions for all members of staff. / The needs of production staff will generally be different from / those of the administrative staff and therefore the courses will / be on separate days. Overtime will be paid at the / standard rate for the time involved. Please complete the attached / questionnaire concerning the most suitable time for your course and / we will try to find times appropriate for everyone. (**129**)

3 Letter from a bank about a new service

Dear Mr Brown

As a customer, you will realise that / we let you know immediately of any new opportunities that / can help you make the important decisions concerning your personal / finance.

A greater proportion of your income is probably being / taken up each month by mortgage repayments. We have taken / a look at ways in which you can cut the / cost of borrowing. This may mean a discount or a / reduction in the interest you have to pay if you / take advantage of the scheme.

The enclosed leaflet explains in / more detail how easy it is for you to save / money. If you are interested all you need to do / is simply fill in the form and return it to / our principal branch as soon as possible. We will then / devise the best package to suit your particular circumstances.

Yours / sincerely (**141**)

31 THE R PRINCIPLE – AR, OR, UR
Exercise 31.1

1 In this country a silver article must have the mark of its maker as part of the hallmark.
2 To save any arguments we will arrange to arrive at the publishing warehouse at 7 o'clock and transfer to your car for the rest of the journey.
3 The flowers were arranged in an original and artistic way and deserved the first prize in the floral art section.
4 It was important to get the patient attended to urgently as he was unable to move his arm which was badly broken in the accident.
5 The south facing garden had a pleasing design and several ordinary stone urns containing flowers were transformed by the unusual use of different shades of orange and yellow.

Exercise 31.2

1 It is most important that the brochure is printed in Urdu as well as other Asian languages.
2 In its supermarkets the organisation used electronic credit control at home and abroad.
3 The arrival in the office of a word processor has made life so much easier for the typist.
4 We will have the electronic typewriters overhauled at the same time as the new word processors are delivered.

Dictation practice
1 Memo from the computer department

This organisation is currently developing a system for choosing word / processors. At the moment, each department makes its own selection / without taking advantage of our specialised knowledge of suitable models /, competitive prices and reliable suppliers. As our productivity is increasing / it is most important that we obtain at least one / word processor urgently and must obtain this from the most / reliable source for quick delivery. **(65)**

2 Letter about a bring and buy sale

Dear Jane

The society has asked me to contact you / to enquire if you can help organise a bring and / buy sale in the town centre in aid of our / local home for animals. In order to advertise this sale / it would be necessary to place a number of notices / in several local papers. We thought you might be able / to arrange this. Perhaps you will be kind enough to / let me know as soon as possible whether or not / you are available to help our charity in this way /.

We should be pleased to know if you can recommend / any other animal lovers who may like to give some / assistance in organising this sale. We know how fond you / are of animals, and thought of you immediately as someone / who would contribute.

Best wishes. **(135)**

3 Response to questionnaire

Dear Sir or Madam

We thank those of you both / at home and abroad who sent in the reader survey / forms. The response was outstanding. We are now in the / process of looking through your comments and, space permitting, we / would like to discuss some of the points raised in / our next edition. At the same time we will announce / the winner of the £1000 prize. At a / quick glance it seems that a majority of you are / in favour of articles that present traditional opinions. However, some / people would like controversial issues raised, but it is most / important that all opinions are expressed.

Thank you again for / completing the questionnaire. **(113)**

32 METRIC MEASUREMENTS
Exercise 32.1

Great Britain went metric in 1975 and since / then children have been taught metric measurements in school. This / can still cause some confusion in the family for what / children take for granted is difficult for their parents and / grandparents to understand. A child thinks of milk in litres / instead of pints and apples in terms of kilograms and / not pounds.

Most mothers still use old recipes in the / kitchen which measure flour in pounds and ounces, but teenage / girls use grams in cookery lessons at school.

When going / on holiday father works out how many gallons of petrol / he will need to cover 300 miles. His son / thinks this is very funny indeed and old fashioned. He / tells dad he should be thinking in terms of litres / and kilometres.
One thing is certain, however, whatever else changes / his father will never accept any change of name for / his pint of beer. (**154**)

FINALE
Dictation practice
1 Memo to company car drivers

Your company has a fleet of 80 cars which, as / you will appreciate, is extremely costly to maintain, run and / replace. The number of road accidents is ever increasing and / however trivial the damage caused the cost is generally high. / With only third party insurance available this cost has to / be borne by your company and, therefore, the need for / greater care at all times is essential. In future, in / the case of any second accident within a 12 month / period which results in cost to the firm, a £ /50 penalty will be charged against the driver. Should the / same driver have a third accident within a 12 month / period a penalty of £100 will be charged. /
From now on regular inspections of company cars will be / carried out by your immediate manager. Please make every effort / to be careful when driving and keep your car clean / and tidy.
Happy Motoring!
Andrew Parker
Sales Manager (**158**)

2 Letter of complaint to a garage

Dear Mr Green
I wish to complain as strongly as / I can about the service which I received recently at / your garage. I booked in my car to be repaired / last Wednesday because the brakes needed attention. I explained to / the manager when I made the booking that I need / my car every day for business and he assured me / that the repair work would only take one day. Therefore / I left the car at your garage, as arranged, at / 8 15 am. When I returned at 5 / 45 pm I was told that the car was / not ready. No explanation was offered. I asked for the / loan of a car overnight but none was available. As / a result it took me 2 hours to get home / by bus. Because I had been told that the work / would be completed in a day I was very angry. / The situation was made worse because I needed my car / early the following morning to keep a business appointment.
I / would appreciate an early reply from you giving an explanation. / In the meantime, I am withholding payment.
Yours sincerely (**189**)

3 Notice to departmental managers

I shall be away on holiday for the next two / weeks starting Monday, July 3rd. If any problems should arise /, outside the day-to-day running of the departments, Mrs / Chang, the financial director, should be consulted. She has the / authority to make any major decisions while I am away /. My secretary has a telephone number where I can be / reached in an emergency. If you are in doubt as / to what constitutes an emergency, perhaps I should explain that / my personal definition would be nothing less than the burning / down of the building or an earthquake!

On the day / of my return there will be a meeting of all / heads of departments at 8 30 am prompt to / consider the first half-year production and sales figures. This / will be an important financial meeting but if sufficient time / is available we may start preliminary discussions on the possibility / of setting up a company creche or nursery for the / young children of employees. Perhaps you could sound out staff / reaction to this proposal during my absence. The initial request / came from the works committee some time ago so staff / reaction should be favourable.

Richard West
Managing Director (**198**)

4 Letter from headteacher to parents

Dear Parent

This school is going through very difficult times / and our experience here at Park Road High is being / shared by all schools in the town. The Government has / told local authorities that there are going to be massive / cuts in public spending and some of these cuts will / certainly be felt in the education service. The economies being / proposed at present amount to thousands of pounds at each / school and the effects of this will be felt right / across the board. No department will escape the impact. Some / departments will suffer more than others. Up to now we / have not been informed of the exact amount of the / cuts but one thing is certain. Every department will have / less money to spend from next year and the first / item to suffer will be the trip to France at / the end of the Spring term. I am afraid that /parents will have to pay the full amount of £ /200. There will be no money available from school / funds to subsidise the trip. I very much regret having / to tell you this because I know that the news / will mean that some children will no longer be able / to go. If this is the case perhaps the parents / concerned would make an appointment to see me to discuss / the matter in confidence.

I would be disappointed if any / child were deprived of the opportunity of taking part in, / what is not simply a holiday, but an educational experience. /

Yours sincerely (**252**)

5 Letter to residents about estate vandalism

Dear Neighbour

No-one seems to have any regard for / other people's property these days, so it will come as / no surprise to you to hear that vandalism has reached / a peak in this town. That in itself is bad / enough news, but contributing to this is the fact that / damage totalling £20 000 was caused in one week / recently on this estate alone.

I have lived here for / eighteen years and I have never known things to be / as bad as they are now. People are afraid to / walk the streets for fear of being mugged – and that / can be in broad daylight. No-one ever ventures out / in the evenings. Most people lock their doors and windows / as soon as they have had their evening meal and / do not go out again until morning. Even then they / cannot be sure that they are safe. Only last / week a gang of hooligans forced their way in by / breaking a small window at the back of a house. / The occupants, watching television, were unaware that young criminals were / ransacking the house.

How much longer are we going to / put up with this sort of behaviour? The police have / plans in hand to put more men on foot patrol / on the estate. This may have some effect on the / problem but we must do more ourselves. That is the / purpose of this letter.

You are invited to a public / meeting of all residents on Friday, February 3rd at 7 / 30 pm in the town hall to discuss forming / a residents association. If you are concerned about the area / in which you live, please come to the meeting. You / will be made very welcome.

Yours sincerely (**287**)

Christmas notice in department store canteen

This is a busy time of the year for staff / in all departments but will those concerned please note that: /

1. The fairy grotto must be attended at all times / when the store is open for business.

2. Will Santas / please make sure they do not wander round the store / in costume. There was an embarrassing incident last week when / two were seen together in the grocery department.

Merry Christmas / to you all.

Frank Jones

General Manager (**77**)

Appendix 1
Special outlines

Listed alphabetically

	Unit		Unit
a	1	discount	24
able/ability	1	electric/electricity	1/8
accident	1	electrician	15
account	2	electronic	26
advertisement	14	enclose/enclosed	11
amount	14	equal	1
and	1	examination	21
anything	10	experience	21
are	1	extraordinary	21
at	3	eye/I	1
attention	15	financial	15
be/been	1	from	1
before	13	general/generally	17
business	4	go	1
circumstance/s	12	government	14
commerce	22	have	5
communication	22	he	1
convenience/	24	immediate/ly	7/8
convenient	24	important	30
day/do	1	impossible	29
department	14	inconvenient	24
development	14	individual	9
difference/different	12	insurance	12
difficulty	15	intention	15
discontinue	24	kind	1

Listed by unit

Unit

Appendix 2
Distinguishing outlines

Listed alphabetically

	Unit		Unit		Unit
amazed	4	amused	4		
became	22	become	22		
behind	8	beyond	8		
came	22	come	22		
cannot	24	can't	24		
century	24	country	24		
ease	9	use	9		
easily	9	usually	9		
exact	21	exceed	21		
excel	25	expel	25		
except	21	expect	21		
farther	18	further	18		
firm	13	farm	13	form	13
has	4	his	4		
lively	23	lovely	23		
new/knew	23	know	23	now	23
on	9	one	9		
perhaps	4	purpose	4		
sample	25	simple	25		
specialised	15	specialist	15		
these	4	this	4	those	4
were	19	where	19		

Listed by unit

Appendix 3
Word groupings (listed by unit)

Unit

5	**Very simple groupings**	as soon as
		as soon as possible
		as well as
		do you
		I am sure
		I must
		it is
		of course
		that this
		they are
		we are
		we shall
		will be
		you will
5	**Able/able to**	he is able to
		I am able to
		we are able to
		we shall be able to
		we should be able to
		you will be able to
5	**Have**	have they
		have we
		I have
		they have
		we have

Unit

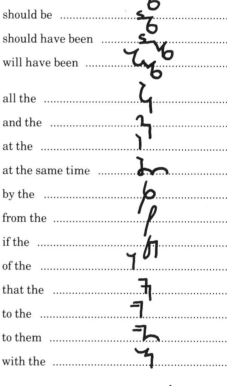

we should have ....

you have ....

5 **Be/been**

could have been ....

I have been able to ....

may be ....

should be ....

should have been ....

will have been ....

5 **The**

all the ....

and the ....

at the ....

at the same time ....

by the ....

from the ....

if the ....

of the ....

that the ....

to the ....

to them ....

with the ....

6 **Would**

he would have been able to ....

I would ....

it would be ....

we would ....

would be ....

would have ....

would not ....

Unit

would we be able to ......

would you ......

you would ......

6 **Word**   last word ......

6 **Nth**   in the ......

in the north ......

in these days ......

in those days ......

7   some day ......

that day ......

with us ......

with you ......

8   I am sorry ......

9   not only ......

10   all things ......

good things ......

many things ......

sending you ......

11   I think ......

thank you ......

thank you for your cheque ......

thank you for your enquiry ......

thank you for your letter ......

vote of thanks ......

we enclose ......

Unit

we think ....

12   at once ....

each day ....

in the circumstances ......

such things ....

too much ....

13   all sorts of things ....

business letter ....

first class ....

first time ....

referring to ....

with reference to ....

with reference to your letter ......

14   Houses of Parliament ....

Member of Parliament ......

in fact ....

in favour ....

last minute ....

last time ....

15   immediate attention ......

your attention ....

16   in order that ....

in order to ....

name and address ....

names and addresses ......

thank you for your order ......

Unit

your order ....

17   Dear Madam ....

Dear Sir ....

Dear Sir or Madam .....

Yours faithfully ....

Yours sincerely ....

Yours truly ....

18   be their/there ....

during their ....

has there been ....

is their/there ....

on the other hand ....

some other ....

that there ....

there has been ....

there is ....

19   all parts of the world ...

Dear Miss ....

Dear Mr ....

Dear Mrs ....

Dear Ms ....

larger and larger ...

more and more ....

more or less ....

more than ....

parts of the world ....

smaller and smaller ....

Unit

	sum of money	
	sums of money	
	this morning	
	worth while	
21	for example	
22	come to the conclusion	
22 **Committee**	finance committee	
	to the committee	
	Social Committee	
22 **Company**	export company	
	this company	
	our company	
22	income tax	
23	no doubt	
	in our opinion	
	in our view	
	in your company	
	upside down	
24	can you	
	for instance	
	I can	
	we can	
25 **People**	other people's	
	several people	

Unit

some people ....

25   I am pleased ....

      it is my pleasure ....

      members of the public ....

      we are pleased to know ....

      we should be pleased ....

      your reply ....

26   under separate cover ....

27 **Over**   all over the country ....

      all over the district ....

      all over the world ....

      over and done with ....

      over and over ....

      over and over again ....

      over the ....

      over their/there ....

      over their heads ....

29   enabled to ....

      unable to ....

31   at home and abroad ....

      most important ....

      word processor ....

Appendix 4
Days, months and seasons; Countries of the EC

Days of the week

	Full form	Abbreviation
Sunday		
Monday		
Tuesday		
Wednesday		
Thursday		
Friday		
Saturday		

Months of the year

January	
February	
March	
April	
May	
June	
July	
August	
September	
October	
November	
December	

Seasons of the year and holidays

| Spring | |
| Summer | |

Autumn	
Winter	
Easter	
Whitsun	
Spring Bank Holiday	
May Day	
August Bank Holiday	
Summer holiday	
Christmas	
New Year	
Half term	

Member countries of the European Community

Belgium	
Denmark	
France	
Germany	
Greece	
Ireland	
Italy	
Luxembourg	
Netherlands	
Portugal	
Spain	
United Kingdom	

About the authors

Meriel Bowers is a highly experienced shorthand and typewriting tutor. She was for many years a lecturer at Huddersfield Technical College where she was shorthand co-ordinator and course tutor for RSA and FTC Teachers' Diplomas. She has been a Chief Examiner for the RSA and FTC Teachers' Diplomas in Teeline shorthand and is still a JEB examiner. She is well-known as an author of previous Teeline books.

Jean Clarkson has been teaching Teeline since 1976 to a wide range of students from GCSE to post-graduate level. She is Chairman of the shorthand examination board of the NCTJ (National Council for the Training of Journalists). She is also shorthand co-ordinator for United Newspapers, and teaches secretaries and journalists on 15 of their newspapers in the North-West.

Stephanie Hall started teaching in 1979. She has been at Sutton Coldfield College of Further Education since 1987, where she teaches Teeline shorthand, typewriting, word processing and information technology. She has taught Teeline to evening classes, YT and day-release students, as well as trainee teachers, and runs many of Heinemann's shorthand seminars.

Celia Osborne has been teaching Teeline since 1968 to a wide range of students, including secondary school pupils, further education and post-graduate students. She has taught the Reuters graduate journalist course and is currently teaching journalists. She is a contributor to Heinemann's **Handbook for Teeline Teachers** and has demonstrated Teeline on seminars and short courses.

Ulli Parkinson has taught only Teeline shorthand, which she has been doing for the past 14 years. She also teaches German and French Teeline. Since 1988 she has been a Senior Lecturer at Oxford Polytechnic. She is the co-author of the German Teeline materials, and has been involved in many other Teeline projects.